Naples
& the Amalfi Coast

by Jack Altman

Jack Altman fell in love with Naples and the Amalfi Coast when he was just 16 and has been returning as often as possible ever since. His home is in Paris, but Italy remains an addiction he cannot kick. Far from satisfying him, 30 years of writing about it, in particular the *mezzogiorno* south, has only whetted his appetite for more.

Above: *cascade of houses above the harbour of Positano*

AA Publishing

Above: *time out for thought outside Naples' Palazzo Reale*
Front cover: *Positano; Galleria del Umberto; young man on scooter*
Back cover: *aubergines*

Find out more about AA Publishing and the wide range of services the AA provides by visiting our website at www.theAA.com

Written by Jack Altman

Published and distributed in the United Kingdom by AA Publishing, a trading name of Automobile Association Developments Limited, whose registered office is Millstream, Maidenhead Road, Windsor, Berkshire SL4 5GD. Registered number 1878835.

Reprinted Aug 2002
Reprinted 2003. Information verified and updated.
Reprinted 2004

A CIP catalogue record for this book is available from the British Library.

A02006

Colour separation: Chroma Graphics (Overseas) Pte Ltd, Singapore
Printed and bound in Italy by Printer Trento S.r.l.

Contents

About this Book

KEY TO SYMBOLS

- map reference to the maps found in the What to See section
- address or location
- telephone number
- opening times
- restaurant or café on premises or near by
- nearest underground train station
- nearest bus/tram route
- nearest overground train station
- ferry crossings and boat excursions
- tourist information
- facilities for visitors with disabilities
- admission charge
- other places of interest near by
- other practical information
- ➤ indicates the page where you will find a fuller description
- travel by air

This book is divided into five sections to cover the most important aspects of your visit to Naples & the Amalfi Coast.

Viewing Naples & the Amalfi Coast pages 5–10
An introduction to Naples & the Amalfi Coast.
The 10 Essentials
The Shaping of Naples & the Amalfi Coast
Peace and Quiet
Famous of Naples & the Amalfi Coast

Top Ten pages 11–22
The author's choice of the Top Ten places to see in Naples & the Amalfi Coast, listed in alphabetical order, each with practical information.

What to See pages 23–72
The three main areas of Naples & the Amalfi Coast, each with its own brief introduction and an alphabetical listing of the main attractions.
Practical information
Snippets of 'Did you know…' information
3 suggested walks and 2 suggested drives
2 features

Where To… pages 73–86
Detailed listings of the best places to eat, stay, shop, take the children and be entertained.

Practical Matters pages 87–92
A highly visual section containing essential travel information.

Maps
All map references are to the individual maps found in the What to See section of this guide.

For example, Positano has the reference 51C2 – indicating the page on which the map is located and the grid square in which the resort is to be found. A list of the maps that have been used in this travel guide can be found in the index.

Prices
Where appropriate, an indication of the cost of an establishment is given by **£** signs:

£££ denotes higher prices, **££** denotes average prices, while **£** denotes lower charges.

Star Ratings
Most of the places described in this book have been given a separate rating:

✪✪✪	Do not miss
✪✪	Highly recommended
✪	Worth seeing

Viewing Naples & the Amalfi Coast

Above: *an artist immortalises Positano's visual delights*
Right: *the best way through Naples' traffic is by scooter*

Jack Altman's Naples & the Amalfi Coast

Driving in Naples?
Inside the city, don't, as they say, even think about it. Use a car only for the Sorrento peninsula, Amalfi Coast and excursions outside Naples. Neapolitan drivers famously describe a red light not as a stop sign but as *un consiglio* (a piece of advice). In acute traffic jams, a daily norm, the same cavalier attitude applies to one-way streets and pedestrian zones.

I love Naples' ambiguity. Unlike more businesslike northern cities, the city evokes the legendary Italian image of warm-hearted exuberance but with an intriguing dark side. Most of Naples' great art is baroque and that goes for the people, too. Baroque art is imbued with a sense of the melodramatic, of movement and a certain tension. This is as true of outraged butchers and triumphant fishmongers along the Via Tribunali as it is of exultant angels and tormented saints in the Church of San Gregorio Armeno. People stage a street-corner *sceneggiata* (performance) several times a day for some choice insult, parking ticket or other catastrophe. Comparing Neapolitans to their monuments is easier now that the *centro storico* (historic centre) is getting a much-needed facelift. But rest assured, for every lovingly restored church or *palazzo*, another is still tottering on in a perversely beautiful state of decay. In Naples, this also is life, sometimes more so than a too artificial renovation. Just as sublime, pizza is treated in its birthplace not as vulgar fast food, but as a noble delicacy, and the tomato as a fruit of the gods.

Naples' long and narrow Via Tribunali

Vesuvius offers the Bay of Naples an enchanting backdrop and an ever-present menace. Pompei, its ancient victim, retains its houses, shops, bakery and brothel. Out in the bay, Capri valiantly protects the charms of its greenery and blue grottoes; while along the Amalfi Coast, a gracious world apart beckons with Ravello's elegant villas, the medieval monuments of Amalfi town, and clusters of houses clinging to the hillside of Positano.

THE 10 ESSENTIALS

If you only have a short time to visit Naples & the Amalfi Coast, or would like to get a complete picture of the region, here are the essentials:

- **Go to the Teatro San Carlo** for an opera or concert in one of the world's most beautiful theatres – or take an out-of-season tour of the interior (➤ 46).
- **Order a Pizza Margherita**, the classical choice, at the Pizzeria di Matteo on Via Tribunali, the destination of gourmets (➤ 75).
- **See the sumptuous Chapel of San Gennaro** in Naples' cathedral where believers see the blood of the martyred saint liquefy every May and September (➤ 32).
- **Sit at the elegant Gambrinus Caffè** with a capuccino and crispy *sfogliatella* pastry and watch the world go by on Piazza Trieste e Trento.
- **Escape the turmoil of city traffic** in the majolica-tiled garden of the Chiostro delle Clarisse at the rear of Santa Chiara Church (➤ 41).
- **Admire Caravaggio's masterpieces** at the Capodimonte Museum (➤ 16–17) and his altar painting in the Pio Monte della Misericordia church (➤ 39).
- **Stand in the Pompei bakery** and look over the ancient ovens at Vesuvius, brooding on the horizon, quiet for the time being (➤ 60–1).
- **Cruise around Capri** in a boat from Marina Grande harbour and explore the island's many grottoes, not just its most celebrated Grotta Azzurra (➤ 13).
- **Take a siesta** under the cooling umbrella pines in the gardens of Ravello's Villa Cimbrone or Rufolo (➤ 22) and then wake up to the stupendous views of the Amalfi Coast.
- **Stroll along the cliffs above Positano** (➤ 69) and go down for a swim at one of the beaches – the popular Spiaggia Grande or secluded Spiaggia del Fornillo.

Top: *reading on the Villa Cimbrone's Terrazza dell'Infinito in Ravello*
Above: *the fashionable Gambrinus Caffè*

Left: *all aboard for a cruise to Capri's Grotta Azzurra*

The Shaping of Naples & the Amalfi Coast

***c*600 BC**
Greek settlers from Cumae (➤ 54) found Neapolis on Pizzofalcone.

341 BC
Romans occupy Campania region.

AD 79
Vesuvius erupts and buries Pompei (➤ 60–1) and Herculaneum (➤ 58).

455
Goths and Vandals conquer Campania and Naples.

661–763
Byzantine Duchy of Naples struggles with Lombards in hinterland.

987
Amalfi archdiocese created at height of city's maritime empire (➤ 67).

1062
Normans launch attack from Capua (➤ 48) to control southern Italy.

1266
Charles d'Anjou installs unpopular French regime.

1442
King of Aragon drives out Angevins to begin 365 years of Spanish rule.

1516
Viceroy Pedro de Toledo ushers in Neapolitan heyday.

1600s
Naples, then Europe's largest city, is devastated by another Vesuvius eruption (1631), the violent Masaniello revolt (1647), plague and an earthquake (1656).

1734–59
Bourbon King Charles VII excavates Pompei and Herculaneum, builds Capodimonte palace (➤ 16–17) and Teatro San Carlo (➤ 46).

1808
The all-conquering Napoleon makes his general, Joachim Murat, King of Naples.

1815
Restoration of corrupt Bourbon regime permits growth of mafia-like Camorra.

Above: *the Aragonese fleet arrive in 1442*
Below: *Garibaldi*

1860
Garibaldi enters Naples preparing incorporation in unified Italian kingdom.

1922
Fascists replace 'popular block' city government with Catholic conservatives.

1943
Allied bombs leave the *centro storico* in ruins prior to invasion via Salerno (➤ 71).

1946
Naples votes to retain the monarchy but also provides the first president, Enrico De Nicola, for the new Italian republic.

1994
Sweeping renovation of historical monuments under Mayor Antonio Bassolino.

Peace & Quiet

Chiostro di San Gregorio Armeno

Naples has few tranquil public squares because the Church appropriated all the best open spaces. This gracious convent-garden is tucked away behind the Church of San Gregorio Armeno, just off the bustling Via Tribunali (➤ 31). Sit on a stone bench in the shade of the garden's wonderful orange, lemon and mandarin trees. In the centre, Matteo Bottigliero's baroque marble fountain is decorated with dolphins, sea-horses and spouting masks, and is flanked by statues of Jesus and the Woman of Samaria.

Anacapri to the Bosco dell'Anginola

Take the chairlift from Anacapri's Piazza Vittoria to the top of Monte Solaro (580m), and hike down through the Anginola woods. The path, steep at first but levelling out, leads through splendidly wild vegetation – over 850 species – past the 14th-century Cetrella hermitage and chapel, and the ruined villa of British writer Compton Mackenzie. Just north of the forest is Axel Munthe's fabled Villa San Michele (➤ 57).

Baia di Ieranto

This exquisite bay at the western end of the Sorrento peninsula has been named a world wildlife site to protect its emerald waters and marine life. The secluded bathing beach can be reached by boat or overland from Nerano.

Take the chairlift up Monte Solaro, highest point on Capri, before hiking back down through the Anginola woods

Naples & the Amalfi Coast's Famous

Pliny the Elder and Pliny the Younger
The eruption of Vesuvius that buried Pompei (➤ 60–1) in AD 79 had two famous witnesses: uncle Pliny the Elder, the historian, observed the catastrophe from what is now Castellammare on the Bay of Naples and died from inhaling the fumes; nephew Pliny the Younger was 18 at the time and recorded the horror in one of many letters that made his name as a writer. He became a famous orator and counsellor to Emperor Trajan.

Above: *a playful moment for ancient Roman historian Pliny the Elder*

Thomas Aquinas

Catholicism's foremost scholar was known to fellow Neapolitan students as the 'Dumb Ox'. He was misleadingly slow in manner and rather fat. Born north of Naples at Roccasecca in 1225, he upset the powerful Aquino family by joining the Dominican Order. He studied in Cologne and Paris before returning to Italy to become a papal advisor and theology professor at Naples' San Domenico Maggiore. As philosopher and theologian, he argued that reason and faith are complementary, harmonious realms. He died in 1274 and was canonised 50 years later.

Right: *Caravaggio was a dashing man in Rome until a fatal stabbing forced him to leave for Naples*

Caravaggio

The couple of years that this violent, brilliant, tormented painter spent in Naples at the end of his life left an indelible mark on the city's art. Caracciolo, Cavallino, Vaccaro and Preti were all Caravaggisti. Born near Milan in 1571, Michelangelo Merisi da Caravaggio fled to Naples from Rome in 1606 after killing a young man in a street brawl. His stark *chiaroscuro* (use of light and shadow) brought an acute, even brutal drama to his religious subjects – five of which were painted in Naples. At 39, he died of a fever alone on a beach in Tuscany.

Below: *Sophia Loren is one of Italy's greatest beauties*

Sophia Loren

She was born Sophia Scicolone in the little port town of Pozzuoli (➤ 54) in 1934. Her healthy sensuality in ancient Roman extravaganzas and earthy Neapolitan melodramas – *Carosello Napolitano, L'Oro di Napoli* – attracted Hollywood's attention. But she worked best back in Italy, winning an Oscar in Vittorio de Sica's *Two Women*, and critical acclaim as a worn housewife in Fascist Italy in Ettore Scola's *Una Giornata Particolare*.

Top Ten

Above: *depicted in the Duomo of Amalfi, St Andrew is buried in the crypt*
Right: *a young painter in creative mood at Paestum*

1
Duomo di Amalfi

51C2

Piazza Duomo, Amalfi

089 872 293

Daily, summer 9–9; winter 10–5

Cafés, restaurants (£–£££)

Corso Roma 19–21
089 871 107

None

Duomo free; Crypt and Chiostro del Paradiso moderate

Arcades of Via dei Mercanti

Pilgrims climbed the long stairway up to Amalfi's cathedral on their knees

Rising above a monumental stairway, the imposing cathedral is the perfect expression of Amalfi's past as a medieval maritime power.

The oldest part of the largely Romanesque cathedral dates back to the 10th century when Amalfi's ships criss-crossed the Mediterranean to ply their trade with Arab and Persian potentates – and occasionally to plunder the cargoes of rivals from Pisa, Genoa and Venice. The exotic tastes of the eastern Mediterranean are reflected in the Arabian-style interlocking arches and majolica-tiled ornament on the church and its 13th-century campanile set at an angle to the façade. The great bronze Byzantine door was made in Constantinople in 1065 by Simeon of Syria and was presented to the city by Pantaleone Di Mauro, an Amalfitan merchant of legendary wealth.

The porticoed atrium at the top of the stairway, rebuilt along with the façade in the 19th century, connects the older Cappella del Crocifisso (Crucifix Chapel) to the main part of the cathedral. Inside the recently restored chapel are fine 15th-century frescoes of the *Enthroned Madonna*, *Christ in Majesty* and the mystic *Marriage of St Catherine*. Completed in 1276, the cathedral was expanded to house the relics of St Andrew in its crypt. The reputed remains of the first Apostle were brought here from Constantinople to be buried under the main altar, designed by Domenico Fontana.

To the left of the atrium, the Chiostro del Paradiso (Paradise Cloister) was built by Archbishop Filippo Augustariccio in 1266 as a cemetery for the Amalfitan aristocracy. Today, the quadrangle is a haven of quiet, the palm trees and slender-columned, pointed arches another reminder of the city's ancient links with the Middle East.

2
Grotta Azzurra, Capri

Revered by the ancient Romans, the cave with its ethereal blue light has been counted among the world's most celebrated natural sights.

Remember to duck your head when rowing in to visit the Grotta Azzurra

The Blue Grotto is not just a tourist attraction to be merely dismissed because of its huge popularity; the mysterious natural light is truly magic. Only special flat rowing boats can get through the mouth of the cave, a mere 2m wide and with barely 1m headroom. The cavern interior is 54m long, 15m high and 30m wide, its waters ranging in depth from 14 to 22m. The grotto owes the unique luminosity of its waters and play of light on the walls to sunlight refracted through the grotto's original opening which subsided some 15–20m below sea level several centuries ago.

In the Galleria dei Pilastri (Gallery of Columns) it is possible to see traces of an ancient Roman landing stage and caverns with stalactites. Around AD 30, Emperor Tiberius built his Villa Damecuta at this end of the island and built the quay and a nymphaeum (shrine to the water nymphs) in the cave – marble statues of marine deities discovered here in 1964 are now exhibited at Certosa di San Giacomo. The smaller Villa Gradola, directly above the cave, was linked to the landing stage by underground passages.

German poet August Kopisch and Swiss painter Ernst Fries rediscovered the cave in 1826 when cruising around with a local fisherman. Delirious with joy, they swam in and out of the cave and then rushed to Naples to spread the news. Almost overnight, the Grotta Azzurra established Capri's reputation as an island of romance.

50B1

Capri

Marina Grande 081 837 0634

Daily 9 to one hour before sunset

None

From Anacapri

Motor- or rowing boat from Marina Grande

None

Moderate

3
Monte Vesuvio

51C2

Parco Nazionale Vesuvio

081 771 7549

Access to crater from sunrise to one hour before sunset.

Café/restaurant (£) at summit car park

Vesuviobus from Piazzale Stazione Circumvesuviana, Ercolano

Ercolano (Circumvesuviano line from Naples)

Ercolano 081 788 1243

None

Climb to crater moderate

Guided tour from summit car park to crater – take a sweater

Osservatorio Vesuviano

081 739 0644

9–1 (groups Mon–Fri, others Sat–Sun)

The peak of Vesuvius looks dormant, but could erupt at any time

This beautiful menace, overlooking the Bay of Naples, last erupted in 1944 and continues to exert its magnetism both on villagers and visitors.

The earliest picture of Vesuvius is from a house in ancient Pompei showing a pretty mountain covered in woods and vineyards. That fresco, now in Naples' Museo Archeologico (➤ 15), was buried in the famous eruption of AD 79. Today, 700,000 people live on the slopes, some in houses only a few hundred metres from the crater. Some 12,000 years after it first exploded into life, it looks peaceful enough – no white plume from the summit and, even up close, just a few steaming fumaroles. But Vesuvius is just sleeping, not dead.

After the Pompei catastrophe, seven major eruptions occurred before 1032 and several minor ones up to the 14th century. The volcano then slept for over 300 years. In 1631, it exploded again, splitting its southern flank and burying 4,000 villagers in molten lava, ash and boiling mud. In recent centuries, the most spectacular eruption came in 1872 when a new cone opened on the north flank. Major 20th-century eruptions occurred in 1906, decapitating the cone and spouting a fountain of gas and lava 600m into the air, and during World War II in 1944, eerily in the middle of an Allied bombing raid.

The volcano today has two peaks, the original Somma (1,132m) and the newer Vesuvio (1,281m), with a crater 600m wide and 200m deep. The road from Ercolano winds through pretty woodland and sombre lava fields to a car park, with a 20-minute walk to the crater. On the way, the **Osservatorio Vesuviano** has audio-visual displays of volcanic activity.

4

Museo Archeologico di Napoli

Proximity to the great Roman sites of southern Italy has enabled Naples to create one of the best endowed archaeological museums in Europe.

Ideally, any projected visit to Pompei and Herculaneum should begin here. In the relative tranquillity of the museum at the top of busy Via Santa Maria Costantinopoli, you can get a sense both of the immense riches of sculpture, painting and mosaics recovered from the buried cities and of comparable treasures brought here from Rome. Like the Capodimonte Museum (➤ 16–17), the Archaeological Museum was originally founded in 1777 to house the private collections of the Farnese family. To these were added findings from the Roman cities buried by Vesuvius, along with other collections from ancient Greece and Egypt.

The best way to tackle the collection is to start on the first floor, with paintings from Pompei and Herculaneum, and work your way down. First-floor highlights include the famous dual portraits of Paquius Proculus and his wife, a splendid Hercules watching his child Telephus being suckled by a doe, and artwork from Pompei's Temple of Isis. There is also a fine 19th-century detailed scale model of the excavated city of Pompei. On the mezzanine floor are the great mosaics of Alexander the Great defeating Darius of Persia, and exquisite bird and animal scenes. Perhaps most famous of all are the erotic paintings, mosaics and sculpture kept in the adults-only Gabinetto Segreto (Secret Cabinet).

The ground floor's most important pieces are the Roman marble statues from the 2nd century BC to the 1st century AD from the Farnese collection. *The Tyrannicides*, *Hercules* and *Dirce and the Wild Bull* are invaluable copies of long-lost masterpieces from classical Greece (5th–4th century BC).

25C4

Piazza Museo 19, Napoli

081 544 1494

Mon–Sun 9–7.45. Closed Tue. Closed 1 Jan, 1 May, 25 Dec

Excellent cafés (£) and restaurants (£–££)

Piazza Cavour

24, 47, 110

Very good

Expensive, Gabinetto Segreto extra

Piazza Bellini (➤ 35)

Audio tours and lectures; advance booking for guided tours. The Gabinetto Segreto can only be visited by guided tour (max 20) by prior booking at the museum. ☎ 84 880 0288.

A Pompei painting (1st century AD) of Paquius Proculus, a prosperous baker, and his wife

5
Museo di Capodimonte

25C5

Via di Miano 1, Napoli

081 749 9111 (recorded information)

Tue–Sat 10–7, Sun 9–8. Park daily 9 to one hour before sunset. Closed 1 Jan, Easter Sun, 1 May, 15 Aug, 25 Dec

Ground floor café (£)

110

Good

Expensive; park grounds free

Audio tours; for guided tours, lectures 84 880 0288

In a hilltop park overlooking the city, the Bourbons' 18th-century royal palace houses one of Italy's most important art museums.

The Museo di Capodimonte brings art and nature together to provide a soothing escape from the city hustle. After decades of neglect, the collections of predominantly Italian Renaissance and baroque painting hang once more in the handsomely renovated rooms of the elegant Bourbon palace. The park's landscaped gardens are a bonus: lawns among groves of pine, holm oak, linden, maple and cedar, fragrant eucalyptus, myrtle and magnolia, and a grand view over the city and Bay of Naples. King Charles of Bourbon (Carlo di Borbone) chose the site in 1739 as hunting grounds and added a porcelain factory (still here). In the palace he hung the art collections of his mother, Elisabetta Farnese, for which the museum was created in 1957.

On the first floor, the Farnese Gallery (rooms 2–30) houses several masterpieces of Italian and Flemish art from the 15th–17th centuries. Highlights include Masaccio's *Crucifixion* (1426), Mantegna's portrait of the 16-year-old Cardinal Gonzaga (1461), Titian's sensual *Danae* (1545, hidden from public view in more prudish times), Parmigianino's exquisite *Antea* (1535, now an emblem of Capodimonte), and Pieter Brueghel's *Parable of the Blind* (1568). On the same floor (rooms 31–60) are the palace's royal apartments showing fine porcelain and objects of decorative art from the Borgia family collection. The second floor exhibits Neapolitan art (12th–18th centuries) with masterpieces from the city's churches.

Above: *Capodimonte Palace was built, in part, with rock hewn from the hill on which it stands*
Oppposite: *in Caravaggio's* Flagellation of Christ, *tormentors kick and tug Jesus into place while tying him to the column*

These include Simon Martine's lovely *St Louis of Toulouse* (1317, from San Lorenzo Maggiore, ➤ 40) and Caravaggio's *Flagellation of Christ* (1609, from San Domenico Maggiore). A third floor displays modern art.

6
Positano

51C2

First-class cafés, restaurants (£–£££) on Marina Grande

SITA between Sorrento and Salerno.

Amalfi Coast (Travelmar 089 873 190)

Via del Saracino 4 089 875 067

Few

Church of Santa Maria Assunta

Via Marina

089 875 480

Daily 8:30–12:30, 3:30–5:30

An afternoon stroll in Positano towards the parish church of Santa Maria Assunta

This elegant resort pours its dazzling white houses and pretty little gardens over the hillside like a cornucopia.

Positano is popularly believed to have been settled by refugees from Paestum (➤ 68) – Greek Poseidonia – hence its name. Certainly it shares today with those ancient Greek colonists an undeniable taste for good living. The only monument of note is the originally Romanesque **Church of Santa Maria Assunta** with a large majolica-tiled dome added in the 18th century. On the high altar is a 13th-century Byzantine-style Black Madonna, and medieval bas-relief carving on the campanile. Positano is a delightful place in which just to hang out, eat the seafood, shop on Via dei Mulini in the fashionable boutiques and to use as a base from where to go sightseeing.

There are plenty of pleasant walks, short and long. From the popular Spiaggia Grande beach, take the cliff walk west past an old Spanish watchtower to the less crowded Spiaggia Fornillo. On the hillside above this beach, climb up to the belvedere for a great view over Positano. Other swimming coves – Ciumicello, Arienzo, La Porta – may be accessible only by boat. The caves here were some of the coast's earliest dwellings, La Porta's having revealed artefacts from the Stone Age. A little further afield, directly overlooking Positano, take the bus up to Montepertuso and walk back down (➤ 69).

7
Spaccanapoli, Naples Old Town

The thoroughfare that splits the historic centre of Naples traces the great moments of the city's story – medieval, Renaissance and baroque.

Spaccanapoli's dividing line follows an ancient Roman main street

Viewed from the hill of Certosa di San Martino (➤ 30), Spaccanapoli slices through the Naples of mansions, churches and university buildings, each with concealed gardens and cloisters, to the Forcella district of craftsmen's workshops. What was once a main artery of ancient Greek Neapolis today changes its name along the way from Via Benedetto Croce to Via San Biagio dei Librai, intersected by side streets preserving the grid plan of antiquity. Piazza del Gesù is the entrance to the Graeco–Roman city, where the Jesuits transformed a 15th-century palace into their Church of Gesù Nuovo (➤ 34). Near by is the fortress-like Church of Santa Chiara and its exquisite cloister-garden (➤ 41).

Palazzo Venezia (No 19) was the home of the Venetian ambassadors. Via Benedetto Croce opens out onto the Piazza San Domenico with its charming café, pastry shop, the Gothic Church of San Domenico Maggiore (➤ 40) and the elegant russet Renaissance façade of the Palazzo Corigliano, now housing the university's Oriental Institute. Via San Biagio dei Librai is dedicated to the patron saint of booksellers, who had their shops here. The 15th-century Palazzo Carafa Santangeli has a marble portal with ancient Roman statues above its carved wooden doors. Inside the austere 16th-century charitable bank of Monte de Pietà is a chapel with a ceiling fresco (1618) by Belisario Corenzio.

25C3

Via Benedetto Croce, Via San Biagio dei Librai

Most churches and several palazzi open daily 9–2

Good cafés, restaurants and pizzerias (£–££)

In the pedestrian zone

Osservatorio Turistico
081 580 8216

Cappella Sansevero (➤ 28), San Lorenzo Maggiore (➤ 40), San Gregorio Armeno (➤ 31), Duomo (➤ 32)

There are informative signposts for principal monuments on the itinerary of the tourist office's 'museo aperto' (open museum).

8

Tempio di Nettuno, Paestum

51D1

Via Magna Grecia, Paestum

082 893 8144

Daily 9 to one hour before sunset

Café (£)

From Salerno (Piazza della Concordia)

Paestum (from Salerno)

Via Magna Grecia 152
082 881 1016

None

Expensive, but includes entrance to museum

Museo Archeologico (► 68)

Scaffolding possible during ongoing restoration

Best preserved of the ancient monuments in the Greek city of Paestum, the 2,500-year-old temple is a marvel of Doric power and simplicity.

Paestum was originally named Poseidonia and this temple was popularly thought to be dedicated to the city's protective deity, the sea-god Poseidon – known as Neptune to the Romans. Scholars now believe it is more likely to have been the temple of Hera or Zeus. It appears to have been modelled on the Greek motherland's Temple of Zeus at Olympia. Colonists from the city of Sybaris (on the south Italian coast's Gulf of Taranto) built it around 460 BC, perhaps 30 years after settling in Paestum.

The excellent state of preservation of this masterpiece of the classical era gives a really complete idea of what most Greek temples were like. Solidly planted on its platform, the temple has retained its architrave, entablature, frieze of metopes and triglyphs, and a pediment supported by a Doric peristyle of six columns on the front and 14 columns along the sides. It measures 20m by 60m. In the interior, a pronaos (vestibule) precedes a vast cella (central chamber) with the nave separated from its two side aisles by rows of double columns. Placed at the front of the temple are altars for the ritual sacrifice of animals, and for placing fruit and other offerings.

The Doric columns of Tempio di Nettuno are the most ancient of classical architecture's three orders

The popularity of Paestum on the Grand Tour undertaken by British and American gentlemen in the 18th and 19th centuries was such that elements from sketches of the Temple of Neptune showed up on the façades of banks, museums and plantation mansions from London to Louisville and from Edinburgh to New Orleans.

9
Villa dei Misteri, Pompei

One of the finest of Pompei's villas, Villa dei Misteri is famous for its cycle of frescoes of lifesize figures enacting the rituals of the Dionysiac cult.

A high priestess presides over the Dionysiac rituals at the Villa dei Misteri

The Villa of the Mysteries stands outside the Porta Ercolano, the ancient city gate to Herculaneum, at the end of Via di Sepolcri, a street lined with the monumental tombs of prominent Pompeian citizens. The villa was a grand country house, the residence of a prosperous gentleman farmer and wine-grower. It was probably built in the 2nd century BC, renovated around 60 BC and then again just before the eruption of Vesuvius in AD 79. It was built on ground sloping down to the sea, then much closer than it is today, with terraces and porticoes offering fine views. Frescoes show the patrician family's taste for the good life in the fashionable Hellenistic manner.

Through the east entrance, visitors reached the villa's spacious peristyle or colonnaded courtyard. Kitchens are off to the south and the torcularium (room for wine production) lies to the north. Two massive wooden winepresses (one reconstructed with a carved ram's head) crushed out the last juices of the trampled grapes into terracotta jars set in the floor.

Residential quarters are grouped around an atrium west of the peristyle. The bedrooms (*cubicula*) are enhanced by *trompe l'oeil* frescoes of elegant arched porticoes opening out to gardens and other buildings. An open living room (*tablinum*) has delicately detailed frescoes of Egyptian deities painted on a dramatic black background. The dining room (*triclinium*) is decorated on three sides with the magnificent fresco-cycle that gives the villa its name: ten richly coloured scenes of a young bride's initiation into the Dionysiac mysteries – a sensual cult much appreciated in the wine-growing region of Campania.

51C2

Via dei Sepolcri, Pompei Scavi

Zona Archeologica 081 861 0744

Daily 9 to one hour before sunset. Closed 1 Jan, Easter Mon, 15 Aug, 25 Dec

Pleasant cafeteria (£) on site near the Forum

Pompei–Scavi (Villa dei Misteri)

Via Sacra 1 081 850 8451

None

Expensive, ticket includes main site and Villa dei Misteri

English-language tours with officially authorised guides

10
Villa Rufolo, Ravello

51C2

Piazza del Vescovado, Ravello

089 857 657

Daily 9 to sunset

Café/restaurant (£–££)

SITA bus once daily from Naples, hourly from Amalfi 6AM–9PM

Piazza del Duomo
089 857 096

Few

Moderate

Ravello (► 70)

Wagner Festival
089 231 432

The romantic garden terrace at Villa Rufolo overlooks the domes of the Annunziata church

With their view of the Amalfi Coast, the gardens of this exquisite 13th-century villa inspired both writer Boccaccio and composer Wagner.

Opposite the Duomo (► 70) on Piazza del Vescovado, a medieval square tower stands at the entrance to one of the most enchanting villas in all southern Italy. The buildings, dating back to the 13th and 14th centuries, rise on hillside terraces overlooking the sea. Arabic influence is apparent in the ornate architecture, especially in the intertwining pointed arches of the cloister-like courtyard. The villa's chapel has an interesting antiquarium of ancient Roman and medieval sarcophagi, funeral urns and architectural fragments.

With their umbrella pines and majestic cypresses, the gardens are heavy with the fragrance of exotic plants. From the terrace, look down over the domes of Ravello's little 13th-century Annunziata church to the coastal village of Atrani. The villa has attracted popes and kings, and it was in these gardens that Giovanni Boccaccio walked with his beloved Fiammetta when escaping from his office job in Naples in 1330. He devoted one of his famous stories for the Decameron to the villa's wealthy owner, Landolfo Rufolo, who resorted to piracy to break the competition of merchants from Genoa.

Over 500 years later, German composer Richard Wagner took the Villa Rufolo's gardens as his model for the Garden of Klingsor in his last opera, *Parsifal*, a solemn religious drama begun here in 1877 and produced at Bayreuth in 1882. Ravello celebrates this inspiration every summer with an open-air festival of Wagner's music performed in the Rufolo gardens.

What to See

Above: *Sant'Angelo on Ischia's south coast*
Right: *sculpture in Caserta palace gardens*

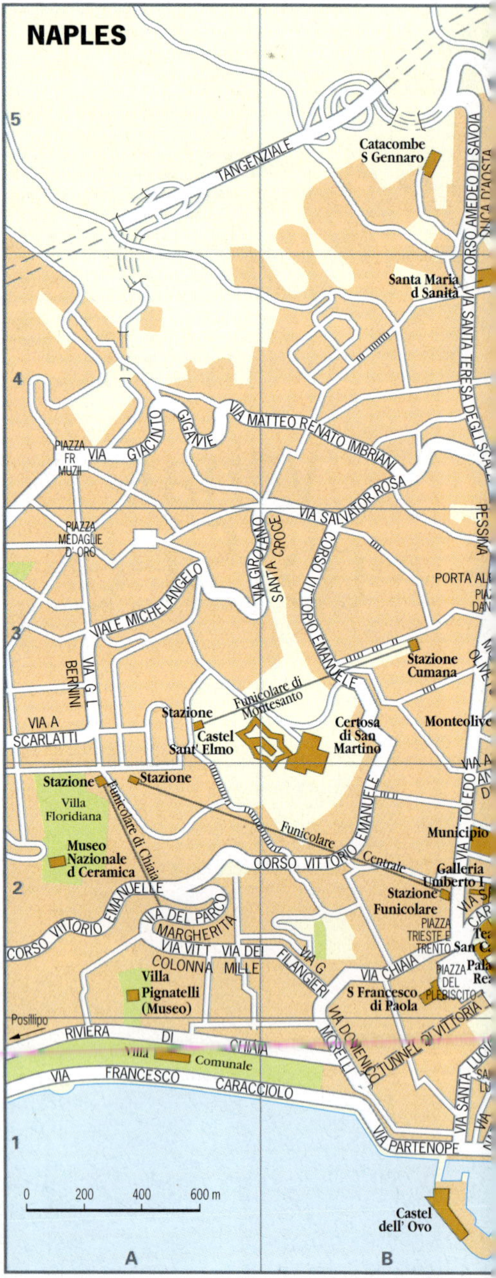
NAPLES
TANGENZIALE
Catacombe S Gennaro
CORSO AMEDEO DI SAVOIA
DUCA D'AOSTA
Santa Maria d Sanità
VIA SANTA TERESA DEGLI SCA
VIA MATTEO RENATO IMBRIANI
PIAZZA FR MUZII
VIA GIACINTO GIGANTE
VIA SALVATOR ROSA
PESSINA
PIAZZA MEDAGLIE D'ORO
VIA GIROLAMO SANTA CROCE
CORSO VITTORIO EMANUELE
PORTA AL
VIALE MICHELANGELO
VIA G L BERNINI
Stazione Cumana
Stazione
Funicolare di Montesanto
Castel Sant' Elmo
Certosa di San Martino
Monteolive
VIA A SCARLATTI
Stazione
Stazione
Villa Floridiana
Funicolare di Chiaia
Funicolare Centrale
Museo Nazionale d Ceramica
Municipio
VIA TOLEDO
CORSO VITTORIO EMANUELE
Galleria Umberto I
Stazione Funicolare
VIA DEL PARCO MARGHERITA
PIAZZA TRIESTE E TRENTO
VIA VITT COLONNA
VIA DEI MILLE
VIA G FILANGIERI
VIA CHIAIA
PIAZZA DEL PLEBISCITO
Villa Pignatelli (Museo)
S Francesco di Paola
Posillipo
RIVIERA DI CHIAIA
VIA DOMENICO MORELLI
TUNNEL DI VITTORIA
Villa Comunale
VIA FRANCESCO CARACCIOLO
VIA SANTA LUCIA
VIA PARTENOPE
0 200 400 600 m
Castel dell' Ovo
A
B
1
2
3
4
5

Parco di
apodimonte
Museo di
Capodimonte
Aeroporto
Capodichino
Observatorio
Astronomica
Albergo dei
Poveri
VIA DON BOSCO
PIAZZA
CARLO III°
Orto
Botanico
Severo
VIA FORIA
CORSO GARIBALDI
VIA ARENACCIA
San Giovanni
a Carbonara
VIA CASANOVA
PORTA
S GENNARO
VIA CARBONARA
PIAZZA
CAVOUR
PIAZZA
ENRICO
DE NICOLA
PORTA
CAPUANA
Museo Archeologico
Nazionale
VIA A
POERIO
VIA FIRENZE
Stazione
Centrale
VIA DEL DUOMO
Duomo
Castel
Capuano
San Paolo
Maggiore
PIAZZA
GARIBALDI
nta Maria
Constantinople
Pio Monte della Misericordia
San Lorenzo
Maggiore
San Maria d Pace
VIA TRIBUNALI
VIA
FORCELLA
onservatorio
di Musica
Cappella
Sansevero
Stazione
Circumvesuviana
VIA SAN BIAGIO
DI LIBRAI
Palazzo
Como
San Domenico
Maggiore
esù
ovo
Archivio
di Stato
CORSO UMBERTO
PIAZZA
NICOLA
AMORE
VIA
BENEDETTO CROCE
San Gregorio
Armeno
PIAZZA
DEL MERCATO
Santa
Chiara
Palazzo
Gravina
Università
Santa Maria
del Carmine
VIA AMERIGO
VESPUCCI
Santa Maria
la Nova
VIA NUOVA MARINA
VIA G
SANFELICE
Capitaneria
di Porto
VIA MEDINA
VIA AGOSTINO
DEPRETIS
VIA CRISTOFORO
COLOMBO
Molo
Beverello
Bacino del
Piliero
PIAZZA
UNICIPIO
Castel
Nuovo
VIA
FERDINANDO ACTON
Bacino
Angioino
Avamporto Ammiraglio
Francesco Caracciolo
Giardini
Molosiglio
Golfo di Napoli
C
D

Naples

Naples is once again taking the centre stage in visitors' affection and admiration that it occupied on the Grand Tour of Europe in the 18th and 19th centuries. Then they came for the baroque churches and Renaissance palaces, for the grand opera and theatre. They came, too, for the colourful street life and for the good food. All this is still here, with the added spice of joyous modern chaos, for the patient and the curious. The Capodimonte and Archaeological museums have regained a grandeur that makes them a match for any museum in Europe. The monuments are looking better than ever. But nobody comes to Naples looking for an immaculate, polished, orderly town. It is a place of real, sensuous life and the people, in their markets and backstreet workshops, have lost none of their natural effervescence.

'Observing things down here in the south, I soon realised it is a purely northern idea to regard as a layabout anyone who doesn't work his back off all day long. On the move or at rest, nobody I saw in Naples was doing nothing.'

JOHANN WOLFGANG VON GOETHE (1749–1832)
Italian Journey

Naples

The city's *centro storico* (historic centre) keeps to the limits of the old Graeco–Roman town, much of it now a pedestrian zone. Almost all the major monuments are located in the narrow triangle formed by the Museo Archeologico, the Duomo (Cathedral) and Piazza del Plebiscito. It is all level going except for the hilltop Certosa di San Martino to the west and the Capodimonte Museum to the north.

To tour the city in easy stages, it is a good idea to keep to three or four separate itineraries. Some like to start with an overall view of the city, from the terrace of the Certosa di San Martino (➤ 30) or Castel Sant'Elmo (➤ 29). Others like to begin in the thick of it, with Spaccanapoli (➤ 19) which, with leisurely stops at the major sights, can occupy one or two full days, depending on the thoroughness of your visits. Similarly, it is possible to spend one or two days exploring the Via Tribunali, taking the circular walk beginning at Piazza Dante and ending at Piazza Bellini (➤ 35). Reserve half a day each for an unhurried tour of both the Capodimonte Museum (➤ 16–17) and Archaeological (➤ 15) Museum.

A stroll down Via Toledo (also known as Via Roma) and around Via Chiaia will provide a mixture of sightseeing and shopping, taking in both the fashionable boutiques and the Palazzo Reale (➤ 38) and Castel Nuovo (➤ 29). But spare time, too, for the bourgeois Vomero neighbourhood around the gardens of Villa Floridiana (➤ 47) and the celebrated Santa Lucia district down by the harbour (➤ 44).

Neapolitans' religious fervour is at its height during the Easter procession through the streets of the working-class Quartieri Spagnoli

Extravagant baroque sculptures dominate the grandiose interior of the Cappella Sansevero

What to See in Naples

CAPPELLA SANSEVERO ✪✪✪

- 25C3
- Via de Sanctis 19
- 081 551 8420
- Mon–Sat 10–8; Sun, public hols 10–1:30. Closed Tue
- Excellent café, pizzeria, restaurant (£–££), Via Tribunali
- R1
- None
- Moderate
- San Domenico Maggiore (➤ 40)

The mystery and beauty of its interior make this chapel one of the city's most attractive and intriguing baroque buildings. It is now a museum situated just behind Piazza San Domenico Maggiore (➤ 40). Built in 1590 as the Sangro family's private chapel, it became a mausoleum for what had become the princes of Sansevero (Severo was a sainted 4th-century bishop of Naples). In the 18th century, the chapel was given its luminous artistic unity by Don Raimundo de'Sangro, leading figure of the Neapolitan Enlightenment, soldier, scientist, man of letters, Grand Master of the city's Freemasons and brilliant patron of the arts.

The Sansevero ceiling has a joyously coloured fresco, *Gloria del Paradiso* (1749) by Francesco Maria Russo, but the outstanding feature is the chapel's sculpture. Left and right of the arch leading to the high altar are Antonio Corradini's sensual *Pudicizia Veluta* (*Veiled Modesty*, a homage to Don Raimundo's mother) and Francesco Queirolo's *Disinganno* (*Disillusion*), an artistic tour de force of a man entangled in a net carved entirely in marble. The high altar has a magnificent *Deposizione* sculpted by Francesco Celebrano. At the centre of the chapel, transferred from the crypt, is Giuseppe Sanmartino's extraordinary *Cristo Velato* (*Shrouded Body of Christ*).

In addition to the chapel's mystic symbolism, male and female skeletons displayed in a lower chamber, complete with meticulously reconstructed arteries and organs, have provoked speculation about Don Raimundo dabbling in alchemy or black magic. A simpler explanation would be his scientific studies of anatomy and his status as a prominent Freemason.

CAPODIMONTE, MUSEO DI (➤ 16–17, TOP TEN)

CASTEL NUOVO ✪✪

The formidable seafront fortress is still known to Neapolitans as the Maschio Angioino (Anjou kings' castle keep), though only a chapel remains from the French rulers' 13th-century castle. The present five-towered structure was built by Catalan architect Guillem Sagrera for Alfonso of Aragon two centuries later. Its entrance, a white two-tiered triumphal arch, is a Renaissance masterpiece by Pietro de Martino and Francesco Laurana. The frieze over the lower arch celebrates Alfonso's triumphant entry into Naples in 1443. Beneath the pediment's river gods, and topped by St Michael, the statues over the upper arch represent the Four Virtues (Goodness, Thought, Knowledge and Wisdom).

A staircase in the inner courtyard leads to Sagrera's splendid rib-vaulted Sala dei Baroni (Baronial Hall). The city council now meets where barons were once arrested – many killed on the spot – for conspiring against Alfonso's illegitimate son Ferrante. A Renaissance portal and a rose window have been added to the Anjou kings' Gothic Cappella Palatina (Palace Chapel). Restoration revealed, in the window embrasures, precious fragments of frescoes (1330) by Maso Bianco and his Florentine master, Giotto. They now form part of the castle's Museo Civico (Civic Museum), along with sculpture by Laurana and Domenico Gagini, and Neapolitan frescoes and paintings from the 15th to 18th centuries.

- 25C2
- Piazza Municipio
- 081 795 5877
- Mon–Sat 9–7. Closed 1 Jan, 1 May, 25 Dec
- Caffè Gambrinus (££), good restaurants near by (£–££)
- 24
- Few
- Expensive
- Palazzo Reale (► 38), Teatro di San Carlo (► 46), Galleria Umberto I (► 33)

CASTEL SANT'ELMO ✪

The massive hilltop citadel, in the form of a six-pointed star, was built by the Spanish in 1537 with tufa stone extracted from its moat. For centuries it was a prison for heretics, revolutionaries and leaders of the Risorgimento movement for Italian unity. The ramparts have a fine view of the city and Bay of Naples.

- 24A3
- Via Tito Angelini 20–22
- 081 578 4030
- Tue–Sun 9–6:30. Closed 1 Jan, Good Fri, 1 May, 25 Dec
- Cafés, restaurants (£–££) around Vomeros Piazza Vanvitelli
- Funicolare (cable-car) Montesanto
- Few
- Moderate
- Certosa di San Martino (► 30)
- Open-air films in the courtyard in summer

Below: *on the Castel Nuovo's triumphal arch, a carved relief of Alfonso I of Aragon savouring his entry into Naples in 1443*

At the Certosa di San Martino, baroque ornament enriches Gothic vaults for a Carthusian order relinquishing its austere life of hair shirts and abstinence

- 24B3
- Largo San Martino 5
- 081 558 6408
- Tue–Sun 8:30–7:30. Closed 1 Jan, Good Fri, 1 May, 25 Dec
- Cafés, restaurants (£–££) around Vomero's Piazza Vanvitelli
- Funicolare (cable-car) Montesanto
- Few
- Moderate
- Castel Sant'Elmo (➤ 29)
- Look for artists at work on figures for *presepe* (Christmas mangers) 84 880 0288.

CERTOSA DI SAN MARTINO ✪✪✪

The majestic Certosa di San Martino (Charterhouse of St Martin) is impressive both for its artistic masterpieces and for the grand terrace views of Naples and the harbour. Consecrated in 1368, the richly endowed monastery was expropriated 500 years later by the new Italian kingdom, but preserved as a museum to present its treasures as a representative history of Neapolitan art. Expanding the original conception of Sienna's Tino di Camaino, better known as a sculptor, 17th-century architect Cosimo Fanzago gave it its predominantly baroque appearance.

An atrium to the church, on the left of the main courtyard, has frescoes by Belisario Corenzio and Domenico Gargiulo of *Henry VIII's Persecution of English Carthusian Monks.* Striking a more triumphant note for the church's Gothic-vaulted nave, Giovanni Lanfranco's ceiling fresco depicts Christ's Ascension. Note among the many richly decorated chapels the Cappella di San Gennaro (first left), with paintings by Battistello Caracciolo and sculptures of the Evangelists by Antonio Vaccario. José Ribera's superb *Apostles' Communion* is in the presbytery, and his *Deposition* is on the high altar. See, too, the beautiful 16th-century inlaid walnut panelled wardrobes in the sacristy.

Worth a visit is the Quarto del Priore (Prior's Apartments), with a spiral staircase leading down to his private garden. The Chiostro Grande (Great Cloister) has a handsome marble fountain in its charming four-square Renaissance arcaded garden. In the monastery kitchens is a popular display of 18th- and 19th-century *presepe* (Christmas mangers), crowded with lovingly carved shepherds, peasants, angels and animals surrounding the Holy Family, the most famous being the *Presepe Cuciniello.*

CHIESA DI SAN GREGORIO ARMENO ✪✪

With its distinctive belfry straddling the narrow Via San Gregorio Armeno, this opulent baroque church is part of a well-endowed convent dedicated to the saint who first took Christianity to Armenia. In 726, nuns fled here with his relics from the Byzantine iconoclastic turmoil in Constantinople. Originally an Eastern Orthodox edifice, the church was rebuilt in the 16th century to meet demands of the Catholic counter-Reformation, notably with a unified nave and four lateral chapels. Flemish artists created the sumptuous coffered wooden ceiling, with its gilded panels and 16 paintings of martyred saints. In the cupola and on the western wall, Luca Giordano's frescoes (sadly damaged by the humidity) depict St Gregory's martyrdom and the transfer of his relics to Naples. Also in a chapel here, since 1864, are the much-venerated relics of St Patrizia, another refugee from Constantinople.

To the north of the belfry, the convent entrance is at the top of a long stairway. The convent's cloister garden is still beautifully kept, fragrant and shady with orange, lemon and mandarin trees. In the middle, Matteo Bottigliero's monumental marble fountain (1733) has exquisite statues of Christ's meeting with the Samaritan woman. In the convent rooms you'll find many opulent artworks, brought in by novice nuns from wealthy families.

The street outside forms the unofficial centre of Naples' thriving manufacture of traditional figurines for *presepe* (Christmas mangers). The workshops sell their carefully crafted wares – miniature shepherds, sheep, dogs, angels, butchers, bakers and pizza-chefs – all year round but Via San Gregorio Armeno reaches a bustling crescendo during the Christmas market. *Presepe* can be seen in their most extravagant form at the museum of Certosa di San Martino (► 30).

- 25C3
- Via San Gregorio Armeno 44
- 081 552 0186
- Daily 9:30AM–noon
- Cafés, restaurants (£–££) Via Tribunali
- Metro Piazza Cavour
- Few
- Free
- San Lorenzo Maggiore (► 40), Duomo (► 32)

A craftsman prepares a traditional Christmas nativity scene on Via San Gregorio Armeno

- 25C4
- Via Duomo 147
- 081 449 097
- Daily 7:30–12:30, 4:30–9:30
- Cafés, restaurants (£–££) Via Duomo, Via Tribunali
- Metro Piazza Cavour
- R2
- Few
- Free
- Pio Monte della Misericordia (➤ 39), San Lorenzo Maggiore (➤ 40)

DUOMO ✪✪

Steeped in the city's long architectural and spiritual history, the Duomo remains the focus of Naples' celebrated miracle, the annual liquefaction of the blood of its patron saint, San Gennaro. The cathedral stands on a site that has been sacred since the Greeks built a temple here to Apollo. Today's neo-Gothic façade (1905) attempts to recapture the medieval character of the Anjou kings' church, itself incorporating two 4th- and 5th-century Christian basilicas. Evidence of these older structures includes the temple's antique marble columns, the basilica's mosaics and frescoes, and the rib-vaulted chapels of the Angevin-Gothic church, along with the baroque art that followed.

The faithful fill Naples' cathedral for Sunday Mass

The cathedral has kept its three original Gothic portals, with Tino di Camaino's 14th-century *Madonna and Child* sculpture over the main entrance. Inside, beneath the ornate 17th-century coffered ceiling, the lofty nave has columns taken from ancient Graeco–Roman buildings. In the left aisle, the 4th-century basilica of Santa Restituta has been transformed into a baroque chapel. To the right of the apse the baptistery has graphic mosaic fragments in its dome. Off the right transept is the 13th-century Cappella Minutolo, with mosaic paving, elegant groin vaulting and a monumental tomb with a gabled canopy over the altar.

Most spectacular of all is the Cappella del Tesoro di San Gennaro, a dazzling baroque chapel that attracts the faithful each May and September to see the saint's blood liquefy in phials kept behind the main altar, along with Gennaro's head. Others are content to admire the frescoes of Domenichino and Giovanni Lanfranco and Ribera's painting of San Gennaro emerging unscathed from a furnace.

DID YOU KNOW?

The liquefaction of San Gennaro's blood happened originally just once a year, on the anniversary of its first occurrence one miraculous September day. Suddenly – cynics say in response to popular demand – it was also observed happening on the saint's feast day in May.

GALLERIA UMBERTO I ✪✪

Among the many quarrels between Naples and Milan is over 'Who has the finest monumental glass-and-steel shopping gallery?'. Milan's Galleria Vittorio Emanuele was inaugurated first, in 1878, but Naples' grand neo-Renaissance Galleria Umberto I, built nine years later, may claim to be the more imposing architectural achievement. Replacing the whole neighbourhood of Santa Brigida, ravaged by the cholera epidemic of 1884, it was conceived by architect Antonio Curri as an affirmation of the new Italian kingdom's modern spirit. It was a natural complement to the prestigious Teatro San Carlo (➤ 46) and Palazzo Reale (➤ 38). The soaring glass-and-steel dome is 57m high, above a central mosaic paving of the Zodiac, from which colonnades branch out, richly decorated with all the polychrome marble and allegorical Graeco–Roman sculptures a prosperous and rather ostentatious 19th-century bourgeoisie could wish for.

In the heyday of Naples' *belle époque*, this precursor of the modern shopping mall attracted high society to the city's smartest cafés, intimate theatres and fashion emporia. Today, the amosphere is more subdued, but reputable jewellers and the venerable Neapolitan designer Barbaro remain. Respectable citizens still gather here at that blessed early evening hour of the *passeggiata*, when Italians traditionally take a stroll to discuss the vital issues of the day – forthcoming marriages, football, politics, football, religion and football.

- 24B2
- Main entrance on Via San Carlo
- Arcade open permanently, shops 9–1, 4–7. Closed Sun
- Cafés (£)
- R2
- Good
- Free
- Teatro San Carlo (➤ 46), Palazzo Reale (➤ 38)

The shopping mall of Galleria Umberto I is a monument of 19th-century eclectic architecture

Ceilings and walls of Gesù Nuovo's lavish interior are entirely encased in polychrome marble

- 25C3
- Piazza del Gesù Nuovo
- 081 551 9613
- Daily 7–1, 4:30–7
- Cafés, restaurants (£–££)
- R1
- Good
- Free
- Santa Chiara (➤ 41), Monteoliveto (➤ below)

GESÙ NUOVO ✪✪

At the west end of Spaccanapoli (➤ 19), on a *piazza* originally just outside the Graeco–Roman city walls, the Jesuits' main church is housed in the 15th-century palace of the Sanseverino princes. (An earlier church, Gesù Vecchio, stands in the university grounds on Corso Umberto I.) Also on the square, the Guglia dell'Immacolata (Column of the Virgin Mary) replaced, in 1747, an equestrian statue of Spain's Philip V, destroyed by the people, who then had to pay for the Jesuits' lavishly ornate Rococo obelisk. The church has kept the Renaissance palace's sober diamond-point embossed façade, adding only the three windows and baroque ornament to the main entrance. The exuberantly colourful interior makes a dramatic contrast. Notice, on the entrance wall, Francesco Solimena's biblical fresco of *Heliodorus Driven from the Temple* and in the left transept Cosimo Fanzago's statues of David and a dismal Jeremiah.

- 24B3
- Piazza Monteoliveto 44
- 081 551 3333
- Mon–Sat 8:30–12, Sat also 5:30–6:30PM. Closed public hols
- Cafés, restaurants (£–££) Via Toledo, Spaccanapoli
- R1
- Few
- Free
- Gesù Nuovo (➤ above), Santa Chiara (➤ 41)

MONTEOLIVETO ✪

Thanks to close ties between Naples' Aragonese court and the Medici and Este princes, Florentine and north Italian art treasures make this 15th-century church (also known as Sant'Anna dei Lombardi) a true museum of Renaissance art. In the Cappella Piccolomini (first on the left), Antonio Rossellino designed the monumental tomb for Maria of Aragon and sculpted the altar's splendid nativity bas-relief (1475). In the Cappella Tolosa are glazed terracottas of the Evangelisti by the Della Robbia workshop. Benedetto da Maiano's charming marble relief of the Annunciazione (1489) is in the Curiale chapel. In the Sagrestia Vecchia (Old Sacristy), with its ceiling frescoes by Giorgio Vasari,is Guido Mazzoni's poignant terracotta statue of the Dead Christ.

MUSEO ARCHEOLOGICO DI NAPOLI (➤ 15, TOP TEN)

Piazza Dante to Forcella

Walk by way of Piazza Bellini from Via Tribunali's aristocratic palazzi, churches and market arcades to the colourful workshops of Forcella. Visit the treasures of San Gregorio Armeno (➤ 31), San Lorenzo Maggiore (➤ 40), the Duomo (➤ 32) and Pio Monte della Misericordia (➤ 39).

After a quick peek at the narrow streets of the Quartieri Spagnoli (Spanish Quarter) west of the Via Toledo off Piazza Dante, take the arched gateway left off the piazza to cut through Via Port'Alba to Piazza Bellini.

Luigi Vanvitelli designed Piazza Dante's monumental crescent in 1757 – now embracing a 19th-century statue of Dante. Students throng the bookshops in the Via Port'Alba arcade and the café terraces of Piazza Bellini, overlooking remains of the ancient Greek city walls (4th century BC).

From the southeast corner of Piazza Bellini, take Via San Pietro a Maiella and cross Piazza Miraglia to continue along Via Tribunali, with short digressions to churches right on Via San Gregorio Armeno, left on Via Duomo.

San Pietro a Maiella convent houses the Conservatorio di Musica. Via Tribunali is the central one of three ancient *decumanus* streets, crossing the Greek agora and Roman forum on Piazza San Gaetano. Fruit, vegetable, fish and meat markets like those in today's arcades have been here for 2,500 years.

Back on Via Tribunali, turn right at Santa Maria della Pace church on Via della Pace. Cross Via Vicaria Vecchia to enter Via Forcella forking to the right across Piazza Calenda to Corso Umberto I.

The names of the side streets here testify to the time-honoured crafts of bustling Forcella: *intagliatori* (woodcarvers), *candelari* (chandlers), *armaioli* (gunsmiths) and *chiavettieri* (locksmiths).

Distance
2km

Time
2–3 hours, with visits to churches and street markets

Start point
Piazza Dante
24B3
R1, R4

End point
Forcella
25D3
R2 on Corso Umberto I

Lunch
Pizzeria di Matteo, a monument in itself (£)
Via Tribunali 94
081 455 262

Neapolitans of all classes now occupy aristocratic Via Tribunali

Food & Drink

Like the best of Italian food, Neapolitan cuisine is simple, savoury and colourful. The tomato is king, the basis of all dishes *alla napolitana*. Historians question whether Naples invented the pizza but nowhere else is it such a gourmet delicacy. And from the Sorrento peninsula and Amalfi Coast comes the great variety of fresh seafood and exquisite mozzarella.

Portions are generous, but in these more health-conscious times, there is no longer the pressure to go the whole gamut of *antipasti* (starters), a *primo piatto* (first course) of, say, pasta, then a fish or meat *secondo piatto* (second course), followed by fruit, pastry, coffee and a liqueur. Instead you can have a light starter, pasta and salad, and then an ice-cream at a nearby *gelateria*.

Starters

Many restaurants offer *crostini* (toasted Italian bread) with chopped tomatoes, onions and olives. For more substantial *antipasti*, try a seafood salad of *calamari* (squid), *polpi* (octopus) or *alici* (fresh anchovies); the popular *insalata caprese*, Capri's salad of sliced mozzarella, tomatoes and basil; or a *peperonata* of green, red and yellow peppers baked in olive oil, onions, tomato and garlic. *Minestra maritata* is a hearty soup of pork or chicken with chicory, usually served the day after a big feast.

A steaming plate of mouth-watering rigatoni

Pizza and Pasta

The purists' classical Neapolitan pizza is the *margherita*. First created in 1889 at Naples' Brandi Pizzeria (➤ 74) for Queen Margherita of Savoy, it bears the coloursof the Italian flag: red tomatoes, white mozzarella and green basil. Variations are quite simply infinite, with seafood, such as *cozze* (mussels), mushrooms, *salsicce* (sausage), scattered with a layer of cold *rucola* (rocket) or the folded *calzone* (pocket pizza), but always with a characteristically fine crust baked in a wood-fired brick oven.

Left: *mussels and clams take pride of place in this seafood platter of linguine*

Naples' favourite pasta dishes use simple sauces of tomato, garlic and olive oil for *vermicelli alla napolitana,* sometimes spiced up with hot red chilli pepper (*all'arrabbiata*), or melted ricotta cheese for the little spiral *fusilli.* Best known of the seafood sauces is *alle vongole,* with Venus clams. More spectacular is the black pasta (*linguine al nero*) in a delicious sauce of finely chopped squid cooked in its own ink.

Fish and Meat Dishes

Best of the locally caught fish are *spigola* (sea bass), *spada* (swordfish), *triglie* (red mullet) or *cefalo* (grey mullet), again served quite simply grilled or with a light tomato and oregano sauce. Two traditional Neapolitan beef dishes are *bistecca alla pizzaiola* (sliced beef in a tomato, garlic and oregano sauce), and *braciolone napoletano* (a hearty and filling meat loaf).

Desserts

Neapolitan pastries can be a delight: try honeyed *struffoli,* iced chocolate *mustaccioli, zeppola* (doughnuts) and sweet ricotta-filled *sfogliatelle,* best with a capuccino at breakfast.

Wines and Liqueurs

The volcanic soil of the Vesuvius vineyards produces some honourable whites, rosés and reds, bottled under the Vesuvio label, as well as the famous *Lacrime di Cristo* dessert wines, fruity and sparkling. White wines from Ravello, Ischia and Capri all go well with seafood. The most popular liqueur, served ice-cold, is the lemon-flavoured *Limoncello,* with Sorrento, Amalfi and Capri all claiming to produce the best. Other locally produced liqueurs are *Mirtillo* (bilberry) and *Finocchietto* (fennel).

Below: *no question in this little fellow's mind as to the ultimate delight of Italian gastronomy*

24B2

Piazza del Plebiscito 1

081 580 8111

Mon–Sat 9–7, Sun 9–8. Closed Wed, 1 Jan, Good Fri, 1 May, 25 Dec

Caffè Gambrinus (££), restaurants Via Toledo (£–££)

R2, R3

Few

Moderate

Teatro San Carlo (➤ 46), Castel Nuovo (➤ 29)

Temporary exhibitions usually open Mon–Fri 9–1:30. Closed Wed

Above: *Habsburgs and Bourbons once strolled through the halls of the Palazzo Reale*

PALAZZO REALE

What began as a palace for the Spanish monarchy came ultimately, with later additions and transformations, to symbolise the new kingdom of a united Italy. The vast palace complex has five façades, the main one being its entrance on Piazza del Plebiscito (➤ 39). Incorporating the Spanish viceroy's Palazzo Vecchio, Domenico Fontana designed the Palazzo Reale in a hurry, in 1600, to receive a royal visit from Philip III of Spain, who then failed to turn up. Subsequently, it was the residence of Spanish and Austrian Habsburg viceroys, then the Bourbon and Italian Savoyard kings.

In the 18th century, Luigi Vanvitelli filled in alternate arches of the main façade's arcade with niches. A century later, Umberto I commissioned eight statues of the rulers of the kingdom to illustrate the course of Naples' history from the beginning to its annexation to a united Italy. They underline the fascinating variety of the rulers' origins: Roger of Normandy, Friedrich von Hohenstaufen, Charles d'Anjou, Alfonso I of Aragon, Charles V of Habsburg, Charles of Bourbon, Joachim Murat of Napoleonic France and Vittorio Emanuele II of Savoy.

The interior's monumental marble ceremonial staircase was given its present neo-classical appearance after a fire in 1837. Today's furnishings for the royal apartments (now a museum), by no means all originals, reflect the style and tastes of the 17th to the 19th century. Two charming survivals of the 17th century are the Teatrino di Corte (Court Theatre) and Cappella Reale dedicata all'Assunta (Royal Assumption Chapel).

PIAZZA DEL PLEBISCITO ✪

The neo-classical harmony of this airy piazza, enclosed in a gracefully curving colonnade, was originally planned in 1810 in resolutely secular style by Joachim Murat, made king of Naples by his brother-in-law, Napoleon Bonaparte. As a votive offering for the restoration of the Bourbon monarchy, Ferdinand inserted, at the centre of the colonnade, the domed **Chiesa di San Francesco di Paola**, inspired by the ancient Pantheon of Rome. Its 17th-century high altar was brought here from the Santi Apostoli church. The piazza's two equestrian statues are of Ferdinand and Charles III of Bourbon.

24B2
Piazza del Plebiscito
Caffè Gambrinus (££)
R2, R3
Palazzo Reale (➤ 38), Teatro San Carlo (➤ 46)

Chiesa di San Francesco di Paola
25C3
Piazza del Plebiscito
081 764 5133
Mon–Sat 7:30–11:30, 3:30–6; Sun, public hols 7:30–1

PIO MONTE DELLA MISERICORDIA ✪✪

A supreme masterpiece of Italian painting rewards a visit to the church of the charitable institution, Monte delle Misericordia, still active after 400 years. On the octagonal church's high altar, Caravaggio's *Opere di Misericordia* (*Works of Charity*, 1606) is one of the most important religious pictures of the 17th century. The Lombard painter uses his mastery of light and shade to illustrate seven acts of charity in one brilliantly grouped composite scene.

The characters come straight from the streets of Spaccanapoli: a grave digger shrouding a corpse; an irritable girl giving her breast milk to an old man in prison; a tired pilgrim; a gentleman clothing a naked beggar; and even the angels accompanying the Madonna and Child look like Neapolitan street urchins.

Take a look, too, at the seven other altars, each devoted to one of the works of charity, the last (from the right) has a remarkable *Liberazione di San Pietro dal Carcere* (*Liberating St Peter from Prison*) by Battistello Caracciolo, a leading disciple of Caravaggio.

Caravaggio's complex allegory of brotherly love, Opere di Misericordia, *is derived from the Gospel of Matthew*

25C3
Via Tribunali 253
081 446 944
Mon–Sat 9–12:30. Closed 1 Jan, Good Fri, 1 May, 25 Dec
Near by (£–££)
Metro Piazza Cavour
R2
Good
Duomo (➤ 32)

25C3
Piazza San Domenico Maggiore
081 441 477
Mon–Sat 7:30–12, 4:30–7; Sun and public hols 9–1
Cafés on piazza (£)
R1 Few
Free
Cappella Sansevero (➤ 28), Spaccanapoli (➤ 19)

SAN DOMENICO MAGGIORE ✪✪

With its café terraces, elegant palazzi and ornate baroque obelisk, the Piazza di San Domenico is one of the most attractive meeting places in the *centro storico*. Entered through the 16th-century marble portal in its fortress-like apse, San Domenico Maggiore church (1283) underwent extensive neo-Gothic restoration in the 19th century. Frescoes (1309) attributed to Pietro Cavallini were recently rediscovered in the Cappella Brancaccio (third right). Left of the nave, the Cappella dei Carafa has a clever *trompe-l'oeil* ceiling fresco of cherubs looking down at a finely carved 16th-century *presepe* (Christmas manger). A mausoleum for the Aragon court, the church has 45 sarcophagi draped in rich silks and velvet on balconies in the sacristy (off the right aisle). Francesco Solimena's ceiling fresco celebrates the Dominicans' *Triumph of Faith Over Heresy* (1709). The Faculty of Theology at the Dominican monastery (closed to the public) attracted intellectuals such as Thomas of Aquinas (➤ 10) and Giordano Bruno (burned alive in 1600).

DID YOU KNOW?

The Dominicans were enthusiastic exponents of the Spanish Inquisition, but were unable to impose it in Naples. In 1547, the 'hounds of God' (*domini canes*), as they proudly called themselves, were forced to halt interrogations under torture by violent street battles.

25C3
Via Tribunali 316
081 454 948
Daily 8–12, 5–7:30
Cafés (£–££) near by
Metro Piazza Cavour
Few Free

Excavations
9–1, 3:30–5:30; public hols 9–1:30. Closed Tue
Moderate

SAN LORENZO MAGGIORE ✪✪

Behind an 18th-century façade is one of southern Italy's outstanding Gothic churches, built in 1266 for Naples' first Franciscan monks by Charles of Anjou. San Lorenzo Maggiore combines French Gothic pointed arches, clustered piers and rib vaulting in the apse and ambulatory with Italian Gothic in the nave's broad walls and truss-beamed ceiling. Among the ambulatory's monumental tombs, notice Tino di Camaino's exquisite shrine for Caterina d'Austria (1323). Neapolitan Giovanno da Nola sculpted the superb high altar (1530) portraying saints Lorenzo, Anthony and Francis of Assisi. **Excavations** in the courtyard reveal the Graeco–Roman food market and treasury which once occupied the site.

Taking it easy on Piazza San Domenico Maggiore

SANTA CHIARA AND CHIOSTRO DELLE CLARISSE ✪✪✪

The 14th-century church of the Franciscan order of Clarissan nuns, also known because of their oath of poverty as the Poor Clares, is especially beloved for possessing one of the most enchanting cloisters in all Italy. With its blind arcades and lofty buttresses, the church itself is quite austere, the façade of yellow tufa stone unadorned except for a rose window above a porch of three pointed arches. Begun in 1328, the free-standing campanile had two upper stories added in the 16th century. Bombing in 1943 destroyed the church's rich baroque decoration, which had been added in the 18th century, and reconstruction restored the original, more sober Gothic style. Among the artworks that survived are monumental tombs by Tino di Camaino for Anjou Duke Charles of Calabria and his wife Marie de Valois, on the right wall of the presbytery. Most imposing of all, behind the high altar, is the huge tomb of Robert of Anjou (1345) for which Florentine sculptors Giovanni and Pacio Bertini showed the king enthroned and also lying on his deathbed wearing a Franciscan habit.

Entered from outside, behind the church, the Chiostro delle Clarisse offers a moment of joyful tranquillity. In 1742, the architect Domenico Antonio Vaccaro divided the cloister garden into four with intersecting vine-shaded alleys. The low majolica-tiled walls and benches show charming scenes, none of them religious, of the everyday life of 18th-century citizens and peasants. Octagonal pillars are decorated with intertwining vines and wisteria, a delightful counterpart in summer to the real thing on the pergolas.

- 25C3
- Via Benedetto Croce, Via Santa Chiara 49
- 081 797 1256
- Mon–Sat 9:30–1, 2:30–5.30; Sun, public hols 9:30–1
- Near by (£–££)
- R1
- Few
- Cloisters: moderate
- Gesù Nuovo (➤ 34)
- Guided and audio tours; occasional lectures and concerts

Majolica-tiled columns in Chiostro delle Clarisse

In the Know

If you only have a short time to visit Naples and the Amalfi Coast and would like to get a flavour of the region, here are some ideas:

10 Ways To be a Local

Take your cappuccino in the morning standing up at a bar.
Call out 'Bravo!' at the Teatro San Carlo, for the tenor; 'Brava!' for the soprano.
Order a pizza in a gourmet restaurant.
Buy a Totocalcio lottery ticket at a street kiosk.
Join in the *passeggiata* on romantic Piazza di San Domenico.
Read *Gazzetta dello Sport* on the terrace of Caffè Gambrinus.

Above: *stand at the bar to drink your coffee*
Below: *first Italian lesson: scooter:* motorino*; mobile phone:* telefonino

Rent a Vespa motor-scooter to get around the Sorrento peninsula.
Sip a *Pantera Rosa* cocktail at the Gran Caffè on Capri's Piazzetta.
Waggle the flat of your hand, palm down, to signal that something is 'not bad, could be better'.
Carry two mobile phones (*telefonini*) in public.

10 Good Cafés and Restaurants

Gambrinus (££) ✉ Piazza Trieste e Trento, Naples ☎ 081 417 582. A venerable and elegant restaurant, handy for people-watching.
Gran Caffè (££) ✉ Piazzetta Umberto I, Capri ☎ 081 837 0388. Join the charming islanders for an apéritif on the terrace after the last day-trippers have left.

Intra Moenia (£) ✉ Piazza Bellini 70, Naples ☎ 081 290 720. A favourite with students and writers.
La Caffettiera (££) ✉ Piazza dei Martiri 25, Naples ☎ 081 764 4243. Fashionable terrace for watching smart people of the Chiaia quarter.
La Zagara (£–££) ✉ Via Mulini 8, Positano ☎ 089 875 964. Try the famous chocolate cake in the shade of the lemon trees.
O Parrucchiano (££) ✉ Corso Italia 71, Sorrento ☎ 081 878 1321 Huge friendly restaurant in a garden setting.
Pollio (£–££) ✉ Corso Italia 172, Sorrento ☎ 081 878 2190. Serves Sorrento's best pastries and attracts big crowds in high season.
La Savardina da Edoardo (£–££) ✉ Via Lo Capo 8, Capri ☎ 081 837 6300. Worth the walk to sample Eduardo's delicious linguine or ravioli amid the orange trees.
Scaturchio (£–££) ✉ Piazza di San Domenico 19, Naples ☎ 081 551 6944. Delicious pastries on one of the city's most handsome squares.
Villa Brunella (££) ✉ Via Tragara 24, Capri ☎ 081 837 0122. Terrace with a romantic view of Marina Piccola.

10 Top Views

- **Naples and harbour** from Capodimonte.
- **Spaccanapoli** from Certosa di San Martino.
- **Bay of Naples** from Vesuvius.
- **Vesuvius** from Santa Lucia.
- **Capri's Faraglioni rocks** from Parco Augusto.
- **Island of Capri** from Sorrento cliffs.
- **Pompei's amphitheatre** from the top seats, facing Vesuvius.
- Along the **Amalfi Coast** from Vietri.
- **Positano** from Montepertuso.
- **Amalfi** from the gardens of Ravello's Villa Rufolo.

10 Top Activities

Canoeing: explore the grottoes around Capri. Marina Piccola, Via Mulo 63 ☎ 081 837 0221.
Diving: good all along Amalfi Coast, even better around Capri. Marina Piccola, Via Mulo 63 ☎ 081 837 0221.
Fishing: no licence required for sea fishing from shore or boat. Amalfi Coast better than Bay of Naples.
Hot springs: thermal treatment, mudbaths, massage at Ischia's Nuove Terme Comunale, Via delle Terme ☎ 081 984 376.
Mountain-biking: Amalfi Coast resorts hire bicycles to explore the back country.
Mountaineering: climb Vesuvius or Lattari mountains behind Amalfi.
Sailing: from Pos'llipo harbours in Naples, or Positano, Amalfi, Capri and Ischia.
Tennis: in major resorts, notably Capri. Circolo Tennis-Yacht Club, Via Camerelle 41 ☎ 081 837 0261.
Walking: self-guided or accompanied walking tours on Amalfi Coast and Sorrento peninsula organised by Alternate Travel Group, 69–71 Banbury Road, Oxford ☎ 01865 310399.
Windsurfing: Amalfi Coast tourist offices advise on rentals. Subacquei Napolitani, Via Caracciolo 2 ☎ 081 761 1985.

If you lack the vocabulary, speak with your hands

Above: *luxury hotels look out over Santa Lucia harbour*

Right: *holidaymakers stroll along the causeway to visit Castel dell'Ovo*

- 24B1
- Via Nazario Sauro, Via Partenope
- Pizzerias and seafood restaurants (£–£££)
- R3
- None
- Palazzo Reale (➤ 38)

SANTA LUCIA ✪

Thanks to the romantic songs of the fishermen and picturesque prints of its waterfront, Santa Lucia was once one of the most popular neighbourhoods in the city. The sailors' church of Santa Lucia a Mare is now set back from the sea since the harbour disappeared under landfill and new construction. The 20th-century promenade formed by Via Nazario Sauro and Via Partenope is lined with luxury hotels, restaurants and yacht clubs, along with a monumental 17th-century fountain, L'Immacolatella, attributed to Pietro Bernini.

On an island joined by a causeway to the Santa Lucia mainland is Castel dell'Ovo (Castle of the Egg), a former military prison now used for temporary exhibitions. Claimed to be named after the Latin poet Virgil's magic egg, the name is more likely to be due to the castle's shape back in the 14th century.

SANTA MARIA DEL CARMINE ✪

The church belongs to a 12th-century Carmelite convent, and has been much changed over the years. The campanile, at 75m the city's tallest, acquired its octagonal drum and majolica-tiled spire after a fire in the 17th century, commemorated by spectacular fireworks on the Carmelite feast on 16 July. The originally Gothic design is submerged by the extravagant baroque and rococo décor of the 18th century. Neapolitans revere the 14th-century Byzantine icon of the *Madonna Bruna* (*Brown Madonna*) behind the altar and, from the same era, a miraculous wooden Crucifixion in a tabernacle suspended from the ceiling. During a military siege of 1439, the Christ figure is believed to have ducked its head to avoid a shell, thus losing only its crown of thorns.

- 25D3
- Piazza del Carmine
- 081 201 196
- Mon–Sat 6:30–12:30, 5–7:30, Sun and public hols 6:30–1:30
- Cafés, restaurants (£–££) Piazza del Mercato
- R3
- Few
- Free

SPACCANAPOLI (➤ 19, TOP TEN)

- 24B2
- Via San Carlo 93
- 081 797 2111
- Opera season Nov–Jun. Guided tours all year Sat, Sun 2–4, outside rehearsal times.
- Caffè Gambrinus (££), restaurants (££) near by
- R2, R3
- Good
- Opera very expensive; recitals expensive; guided tours moderate
- Palazzo Reale (➤ 38), Galleria Umberto I (➤ 33)
- Weekend afternoon guided tour of auditorium

TEATRO SAN CARLO

In 1737, Charles of Bourbon commissioned this opera house, dedicated to his patron saint, to rival those of Venice and Rome. It was part of an ambitious building programme that included the Museo Archeologico (➤ 15) and the palaces of Capodimonte (➤ 16–17) and Caserta (➤ 49). Coming at a time when Naples was the third largest city in Europe (after London and Paris), it proved to be a magnificent monument for the city's most popular artistic expression, the *bel canto*.

Building contractor-cum-impresario Angelo Carasale completed the work in just 300 days, carrying out Giovanni Antonio Medrano's opulent design in gold, silver and blue, the colours of the Bourbon royal household. To give the royal guests easy access to the theatre, it was built on to the Palazzo Reale. The backdrop could originally be opened out on to the palace gardens. With its 184 boxes arranged in six tiers, the San Carlo still seats an audience of 3,000, probably remaining the biggest opera house in Europe.

In 1810, in keeping with the French taste of the time, Napoleon's Joachim Murat had Tuscan architect Antonio Niccolini add a new neo-classical façade. Destroyed by fire six years later, it was faithfully rebuilt by Niccolini for the Bourbon King Ferdinand. Composers Rossini and Donizetti both wrote and conducted operas for the San Carlo, and in 1835 Donizetti directed the world première of his hyper-romantic tragedy, *Lucia di Lammermoor*. The guided tour will show you the architecture, but only a performance can convey the essential fourth dimension, the fervent Neapolitan audience.

Some of the most beautiful voices in the world have been heard from the six golden tiers of Teatro San Carlo

DID YOU KNOW?

Gioacchino Rossini, who wrote over 40 operas, despite a reputation for incurable laziness, was 'imprisoned' in a Naples palazzo to force him to meet his Teatro San Carlo contract in 1816. After months of carousing without producing a note, in two weeks behind locked doors he composed his *Otello*, the standard work until Verdi's superseded it 70 years later.

Villa Floridiana offers a tranquil setting for its priceless collection of porcelain and glassware

VILLA FLORIDIANA

The villa and its handsome gardens, now one of Naples' most attractive public parks, were designed in 1819 by Antonio Nicollini as a summer palazzina for Ferdinand of Bourbon's wife, Lucia Migliaccio, Duchess of Floridia. Amid groves of oak, pine and lemon trees, and magnificent beds of camellias, the neo-classical villa houses the **Museo Duca di Martina**'s impressive collection of European, Chinese and Japanese ceramics. Placido de Sangro, Duke of Martina, was in the 1880s a passionate collector of all manner of *objets d'art* picked up on his travels around Europe – glassware, enamelwork, coral, bronzes – but, above all, it is his porcelain and majolica that make this museum outstanding. It ranges from Spanish–Moorish to Italian Renaissance, from finest German Meissen to French Sèvres, including one delightful piece from the Rambouillet palace dairy, a cup of unmistakable shape known as *Le sein de la Reine* (the Queen's Breast), without identifying the queen.

- 24A2
- Via Domenico Cimarosa 77
- Daily 9 to one hour before sunset
- Cafés and restaurants (£–££) around Piazza Vanvitelli
- Metro Piazza Vanvitelli, Funicolare (cable-car) di Chiaia
- Good
- Free
- Certosa di San Martino (➤ 30)

Museo Duca di Martina

- 081 578 8418
- Tue–Sun 9–2
- Moderate

VILLA PIGNATELLI

This noble neo-classical Doric-columned villa, built in 1826, was the home of the Actons, a Naples-born family of British origin who were statesmen and counsellors in the service of the Neapolitan Bourbon kings. The villa passed on to the German Rothschilds and Italian aristocracy, but the gardens retained their English landscaping, enriched by a colourful array of Mediterranean and sub-tropical flowers, shrubs and trees. The villa stages concerts and temporary art exhibitions while a Museo delle Carrozze (carriage museum) is housed in a separate building in the park.

- 24A2
- Riviera di Chiaia 200
- 081 669 675
- Tue–Sun 9–2, also Sat 2:30–4:30
- Café, restaurant (£–£££) near by
- R3
- Few
- Cheap

It was in this amphitheatre in ancient Capua that Spartacus and other gladiator-slaves fought before their revolt in 73 BC

What to See Around Naples

CAPUA

Present-day Capua lies on a bend of the Volturno river 5km southeast of ancient Capua – and 34km north of Naples. After the original town of Capua was destroyed by Arab invaders in the 9th century, survivors rebuilt their homes on the site of their ancient river port, Casilinum. Ancient Capua, now known as Santa Maria Capua Vetere with a population of 33,000, was an Etruscan colony and often took an independent stance towards Rome. In 216 BC Capua gave hospitality to Hannibal's Carthaginian armies; and, in 73 BC, it was at Capua's gladiator school that Spartacus launched his famous slave revolt. The remains of ancient Capua's **Anfiteatro Campano** (amphitheatre), the scene of Spartacus' uprising, show it to have measured 169m by 139m with four floors reaching a height of 46m. This made it second in size only to the Colosseum in Rome. Other remains include the Arco di Adriano (Hadrian's Arch), honouring the emperor for having restored the amphitheatre, and the Mitreo (Mithraeum), a shrine to the Persian god Mithras, a virile cult popular with Roman soldiers. On the façade of the modern town's Palazzo Municipale in Piazza dei Giudici are the busts of seven deities taken from the amphitheatre. The ancient monument also furnished massive stone blocks for the right wall of the Church of the Annunziata.

The important archaeological finds are in present-day Capua's **Museo Campano**. Of particular interest are the votive offerings of fertility statuettes depicting mothers holding babies, some 200 in all.

50B3

Anfiteatro Campano
Piazza 1 Ottobre 1869
Tue–Sun 9 to one hour before sunset
CTP from Piazza Garibaldi
Piedimonte Matese to Santa Maria Capua Vetere
None
Cheap

Museo Campano
Via Roma 68
082 396 1402
Tue–Sat 9–1:30, Sun 9–1
Gran Caffè, Piazza dei Giudici 1 082 396 1623
Municipio, Piazza Giudici, Capua 082 396 1322
Few
Cheap

DID YOU KNOW?

The Oscans, a sensual, fun-loving Italic tribe who founded Capua (and Pompei), are recognised as creators of the broad theatrical farce that grew into *commedia dell'arte*, long popular in Naples. In fact, etymologists believe the word 'obscene' may be derived from their name.

CASERTA

Lying on the edge of a plain just 30km north of the regional capital, in good hunting country, Caserta offered Charles of Bourbon a perfect counterpart to the Versailles of Louis XIV. He ordered the construction of the huge **Palazzo Reale**, with its vast gardens, fountains and cascades, designed by Luigi Vanvitelli in 1752. The palace's five floors form a rectangular block 184m wide and 247m long with a total of 1,200 rooms. Only the second-floor royal apartments are open to the public, but they provide a lesson in what to expect from overweening power. With a classic Italian sense of theatre, the ceremonial staircase divides in two as it approaches the apartments' grandiose vestibule, an octagonal marble arcaded hall. The great hall, the Salone d'Alessandro, is furnished in the Empire style of the Bourbons' sworn enemy, Napoleon. The Throne Room is decorated with 44 medallions of the kings of Naples from the first Normans to the last Bourbon of 1859.

The **park**, also designed by Vanvitelli, has the same theatricality as the palace. In perfect geometrical form, the swansong of French landscaping before the more romantic English style took over in the 19th century, its central axis slopes 3km down through fish ponds and fountains to the great Cascata da Diana. As an amusing counterpoint, the Giardino Inglese (English Garden), with artificial ruins around a swan lake was added by Vanvitelli's son, Carlo.

For lunch, and a change of pace, drive 10km up to the perfectly preserved medieval hilltop village of Caserta Vecchia.

50B3

Palazzo Reale

Piazza Carlo III, Caserta
082 327 7111
Tue–Sun 8:30–7
La Castellana, Via Torre 4, Caserta Vecchia (10km) 0823 371 230
CTP from Piazza Garibaldi
Stazione Centrale, Naples, to Caserta-Reggia (Palace)
In Royal Palace 082 332 6300
Few
Moderate

Park

Tue–Sun 8:30–2:30
Moderate
Guided tours of the Giardino Inglese 9:30–1:30

One of huntress Diana's nymphs drying off after a shower under the cascade in the Caserta Palace gardens

Above: *local produce for sale*
Right: *boats moored in the Bay of Naples*

Above: *enjoying lunch at a café in Amalfi*

A MARECHIARO
Salv. di Giacomo
quanno sponta la
luna a Ma-re-chia-ro
Paolo Tosti

Bay of Naples

The beauty of the Bay of Naples is almost too perfect – the bold curve around the city itself, the romantic profile of Mount Vesuvius, and beyond, the rugged Sorrento peninsula, all flanked by the sentinel islands of Capri and Ischia. But nature and man have intervened, like red chilli peppers startling the palate in an *arrabbiata* pasta sauce: to the west the vaporous fumaroles of the Campi Flegrei, to the east urban monstrosities around the ancient ruins of Pompei and Herculaneum. Yet beauty prevails. Away from the metropolitan sprawl, the clear coastal waters are suffused with the bay's unique luminosity to produce truly emerald green and sapphire blue grottoes. And the splendours of Roman antiquity survive, from the Pompeian houses and shops to the imperial villas of Capri.

'Luckily the fire stopped just short of us. The shadows and the ash returned, thick and heavy. From time to time, we arose to shake it off, otherwise we would have been covered and crushed by its weight'

PLINY THE YOUNGER
Witnessing the volcanic eruption
that buried Pompei
Letters AD 47

Opposite: *the first lines of a famous song celebrate the moon over Marechiaro*

Remains of an ancient Roman market in the port city of Pozzuoli

What to See Around the Bay of Naples

CAMPI FLEGREI AND THE SPA TOWNS ✪✪

Volcanic activity in the Phlegrean (Greek for 'burning') Fields fascinated ancient Romans and later European aristocrats on the Grand Tour. They came hoping for a (mild) eruption and to bathe in the hot springs. The resorts retain traces of their Roman past and attract Neapolitans escaping the city bustle. Agnano Terme, now a Naples suburb, has spa facilities built into caves next to the crater of an extinct volcano – and within the crater there is weekend horseracing at the **Ippodromo**. Growing in another crater just to the north, are the Astroni woodlands of oak, chestnut, elm and poplar; once used by King Alfonso of Aragon for hunting, they are now a nature reserve. Pozzuoli, originally a Greek trading port (in the 6th century BC), is the region's largest town. It has a large **Roman amphitheatre** and was birthplace of Sophia Loren (➤ 10). In the slumbering **Solfatara** crater on the eastern outskirts, mudpools bubble and fumaroles give off sulphurous steam. Seismic upheaval in 1970 forced evacuation of the town's historic Rione Terra district.

Baia and Bacoli remain the fashionable seaside resorts they were for ancient Romans. Neapolitans come for the seafood restaurants, but a further attraction is the ruin of an imperial villa in Baia's **Parco Archeologico**. Cuma, one of the western Mediterranean's oldest Greek colonies (750 BC), has romantic ruins overgrown with vines and olive trees, two Greek temples, a Roman forum and, most famous of all, the Antro della Sibilla (Cave of the Cumaean Sybil), from which the prophetess dispensed her wisdom.

DID YOU KNOW?

The usual seismic activity in the Campi Flegrei is not a full-blown earthquake registering high on the Richter Scale, but a sneaky quake that slowly, but with devastating effect, heaves the earth up and down. The scientists call it 'bradyseism' – a slow quake.

50B3
Pozzuoli, Bacoli, Baia (£–££)
Ferrovia Cumana from Montesanto (Naples)
Via Campi Flegrei, Pozzuoli ☎ 081 526 5068

Ippodromo di Agnano
Jun–Sep, Sat, Sun first race 8PM; Oct–May, Sat, Sun first race 3PM

Anfiteatro Flavio (Roman amphitheatre)
✉ Via Terracciano 75, Pozzuoli
☎ 081 526 2341
Daily 9 to one hour before sunset
None
Cheap

Solfatara
✉ Via Solfatara 161, Pozzuoli
☎ 081 526 2341
Daily 8:30 to one hour before sunset
None
Cheap

Parco Archeologico di Baia
✉ Via Fusaro 35
☎ 081 855 3285
Daily 9 to one hour before sunset
None
Cheap

Around the Sorrento Peninsula

This tour takes in the peninsula's rugged north coast, the plains of citrus groves and mountains of the interior, with spectacular views over both the Bay of Naples (➤ 53) and the west end of the Amalfi Coast (➤ 66).

On the A3 autostrada *from Naples, fork south to the Castellammare di Stabia exit to start the drive. From Castellammare's Villa Quisisanat, S145 hairpins up Monte Faito before heading back down to the coast to Vico Equense.*

Castellammare di Stabia (ancient *Stabiae*) has been a renowned spa resort since Roman antiquity. It was buried by the Vesuvius eruption of AD 79, but was quickly rebuilt. It has a medieval castle and the Antiquarium Stabiae exhibiting archaeological finds. On Monte Faito, woods of ash, chestnut and pine alternate with meadows, vineyards and olive groves. Earthquake and war destroyed all Vico Equense's historic treasures, apart from a Gothic church and medieval gate.

From Vico, the road continues to Meta where it forks west to Sant'Agnello and Sorrento (➤ 63). At the west end of the ever-popular resort, S145 turns left up to Sant'Agata.

For those not lunching in Sorrento, Sant'Agata sui due Golfi is home to one of Italy's most prestigious – and expensive – gourmet restaurants (Don Alfonso, ➤ 76) plus, absolutely free, a magnificent view over both the Bay of Naples and the Bay of Salerno.

From Sant'Agata an optional detour down to the peninsula's south coast at Marina di Cantone will add 45-minutes' drive each way before continuing to the end of the drive at Positano (➤ 18).

Marina di Cantone is a little beach resort much appreciated by the sailing fraternity for its seafood restaurants. The road east to Positano offers a first glimpse of the charms of the Amalfi Coast.

Distance
85–110km, depending on detours

Time
Allow a day

Start point
Castellammare di Stabia
51C2

End point
Positano
51C2

Lunch
O'Parrucchiano (£–££)
Corso Italia 71, Sorrento
081 878 1321

The craggy shoreline of the Amalfi Coast viewed from the Sorrento peninsula

Capri

Capri – age cannot wither her nor package tours stale her infinite variety. The colours and fragrance of Mediterranean and sub-tropical vegetation, elegant patrician villas, romantic Roman ruins amid mountain greenery, overlooking blue, blue waters washing secluded coves and mysterious grottoes – all seduce the willing visitor. Emperor Tiberius was charmed into building 12 villas here; an heir to the Krupp steel fortune turned away from the family business; and countless painters and poets have forgotten to go home.

50B1
Marina Grande-Capri; Marina Grande-Anacapri; Capri-Anacapri; Anacapri-Grotta Azzurra
Caremar (Naples, Sorrento, Positano) 081 551 3882
Few
Capri permits personally owned cars year round, hire cars from 1 Nov to 1 April. Best form of transport is the local bus or boat.

Hydrofoils and ferries serve Capri from Naples, Sorrento and Positano. Naples' hydrofoil takes 35 minutes, the cheaper ferry 80 minutes, but with it you get the chance to see dolphins pilot the boat across the bay and, for newcomers it offers a more charming first view of the island from the deck.

What to See on Capri

ANACAPRI ✪✪

50B1
Chairlift: Mar–Oct 9:30 to one hour before sunset; Nov–Apr 10:30–3. Closed Tue
Via G Orlandi 081 837 1524

The island's second (Ana- means 'other'), quieter town, with white houses halfway up the slopes of Monte Solaro, is served by a scenic chairlift from Piazza Vittoria (➤ 9). Via Capodimonte, lined with tourist shops, leads to Villa San Michele (➤ 57). On Piazza San Nicola, the baroque church of San Michele has fine majolica-tiled paving showing the *Garden of Eden* (1761) by Francesco Solimena.

CAPRI TOWN ✪✪

50B1
Piazza Umberto I 081 837 0686

Dominating the eastern side of the island, the capital has at its centre one of the Mediterranean's most fashionable meeting places, Piazza Umberto I, better known as the Piazzetta, more courtyard than square. Its cafés look across to a sturdy clock tower and the quaint Moorish-baroque Santo Stefano church. Like Venice in July, the town offers an escape from the madding crowds just two minutes away in its maze of little arcaded lanes.

Capri's little Piazzetta is one of the best-known squares in Italy, a must for people-watching

GROTTA AZZURRA (➤ 13, TOP TEN)

Above: *the view over the Molo di Ponente and Molo di Levante jetties in Capri's main harbour*

PARCO AUGUSTO AND VIA KRUPP ✪✪

The Parco Augusto, at the southern edge of Capri Town, offers splendid panoramas over the Certosa di San Giacomo, the harbour of Marina Piccola and the great Faraglioni rocks out in the bay. Just right of the gardens is a bust of Lenin, who visited his writer friend Maxim Gorky's villa in 1910. Starting under the park's bridge, the spectacular Via Krupp winds dizzily down to the sea with magnificent coastal views on the way. It was built by Friedrich Alfred Krupp (1854–1902), playboy son of a steel magnate who was believed to have committed suicide when accused of organising orgies in an island grotto.

- 50B1
- Via Matteotti
- Daily 9 to one hour before sunset

VILLA JOVIS ✪✪✪

Best preserved of Emperor Tiberius's dozen villas on Capri, this grand residence sprawls across the island's eastern promontory. Built around three vast cisterns for storing rainwater, the imperial apartments are on the north side, bath houses to the south, and kitchens and servants' quarters to the west. The view across the Bay of Naples to Vesuvius was the emperor's parting gift to enemies hurled over the precipice known as Salto di Tiberio (Tiberius Jump), to the right of the villa entrance.

- 50B1
- Via A Maiuri
- 081 837 5308
- Daily 9 to one hour before sunset

VILLA SAN MICHELE ✪✪

A short walk from Anacapri's Piazza Vittoria, this villa is a charming monument to Axel Munthe (1857–1949), Swedish author of the perennial bestseller, *The Story of San Michele*. Built by the writer-physician himself, the house is an eclectic mix of styles, combining baroque furnishings and Roman antiquities. It grew out of a villa and chapel which themselves stand on ruins from the Roman era. The garden, with its handsome terraces and trellised arches, commands a fine view over the Bay of Naples.

- 50B1
- Viale Axel Munthe 3
- 081 837 1401
- Apr–Oct 9–6; Nov–Mar 10:30–3:30

The Bay of Naples continued

- 50B2
- Scavi (excavations), Corso Ercolano 123
- 081 739 0963
- Daily 9 to one hour before sunset
- Cafés (£) near tourist office
- Circumvesuviana (from Naples or Sorrento) to Ercolano
- Via IV Novembre 82 081 788 1243
- Few
- Moderate
- Guided tours available

Right: *in the Casa di Nettuno mosaic, Amphitrite coyly turns away from the advances of her lover, Neptune*

Below: *many of Herculaneum's houses weathered the volcanic eruption better than those at Pompei*

HERCULANEUM ✪✪

In an enclosure within the modern town of Ercolano, Herculaneum is less immediately spectacular than Pompei (➤ 60–1), but more compact and generally better preserved. Even a short visit gives a clear idea of what an ancient Roman town looked like. Whereas the eruption of AD 79 destroyed Pompei with volcanic cinders, it buried Herculaneum under rivers of hot mud, creating a protective crust up to 20m thick. Houses survived with one and even two upper storeys and woodwork intact, though they were stripped of paintings by Bourbon excavators in the 18th century. The excavated part – much, perhaps most, still buried under the modern town – suggests a leisured aristocratic community compared to more commercially oriented Pompei.

The town's grid plan runs south from its main street, Decumanus Maximus, to a promontory once much closer to the sea. The bay view made this a choice neighbourhood. The large Casa dei Cervi, House of the Stags (Cardus V), is named after its sculpture of stags being attacked by dogs. It also depicts a very drunk Hercules. On Cardus IV are impressive multiple family dwellings with two upper floors: Casa del Tramezzo di Legno (House of the Wooden Partition) and Casa Graticcio (Lattice House), with a balcony overlooking the street. Further north, Casa del Mobilo Carbonizzato (House of the Charred Furniture) retains a divan bed and a small table. Next door, the wine merchant's Casa di Nettuno (House of Neptune) has a miraculously preserved ground-floor counter, utensils, shelves of wine jars, and in its courtyard a pretty green and blue mosaic of Neptune and his wife, Amphitrite.

ISCHIA

As Pithecusa (Monkey Island), Ischia was the Greek settlers' first Italian foothold (800 BC) before they went on to colonise Cuma 50 years later (➤ 54). Geologically, the island is a volcanic extension of the Campi Flegrei (➤ 54) via the two stepping-stone isles of Procida and tiny Vivara, a nature reserve. The only volcanic activity apparent today is the hot springs, notable at the fashionable resorts of Casamicciola Terme and Lacco Ameno. Both on the north coast and enjoying a particularly mild climate, they have fine sandy beaches and excellent watersports facilities.

Lacco Ameno's Museo Archeologico (under restoration) displays finds from the ancient Greek settlement, including 'Nestor's Cup' with the oldest known inscription of Greek verse, dating from the time that Homer's epics were first written down.

Near the pretty little south coast fishing village of Sant'Angelo is Spiaggia del Maronti, a beach pockmarked with volcanic fumaroles merrily spouting steam.

The main harbour town of Ischia Porto is a largely 18th-century development, with Terme Comunali (public spa facilities) just beyond the port. The late afternoon *passeggiata* takes place on Corso Vittoria Colonna, past the boutiques, cafés, restaurants and majolica-domed Church of Santa Maria delle Grazie.

Fast-growing Forio is the most popular west coast resort, with its landmark silhouette of the gleaming white 16th-century Santuario del Soccorso. Just outside town, British composer Sir William Walton built his villa, **La Mortella**, famous for its garden planted with magnolia, camellia, yucca, ginger and palm trees.

50A2

From major towns, island circuit 2½ hrs, CD buses clockwise, CS counter-clockwise

Hydrofoil from Naples (Molo Beverello) to Ischia Port or Forio, Alilauro ☎ 081 552 2838

Tourist Information, Via Iasolino ☎ 081 991 146

La Mortella

Via F Calise 35, Forio

081 986 237

Tue, Thu, Sat, Sun 9–7

Few

Cheap

A moment of quiet in the harbour of Ischia Porto

Cupid watches over Venus on her seashell in this wall-painting in a Pompei garden

- 51C2
- Pompei Scavi, Porta Marina
- 081 861 0744
- Daily 9 to one hour before sunset. Closed 1 Jan, Easter Mon, 15 Aug, 25 Dec
- Pleasant cafeteria (£) near the Forum
- Circumvesuviana: Pompei–Scavi (Villa dei Misteri)
- Via Sacra 1 081 850 8451
- None
- Expensive: ticket includes main site and Villa dei Misteri (➤ 21)
- English-language tours with official guides; for self-guided tours site map available from ticket office.

POMPEI ✪✪✪

This is the stuff of ancient Roman daily life. We are its privileged witnesses today, thanks to the town's tragic burial under volcanic ash in AD 79 and its miraculous preservation until excavations began in 1748. Along with its temples, town hall, theatres and other public buildings, the shops and houses are still here, the market, the bakery and brothel, the wine shop and grocery store – and poignant remains of people trapped in the catastrophe. Once located much closer to the sea than it is today, at the mouth of the Sarno River, Pompei prospered as a distribution centre for farming produce – wheat, olives, table grapes and wine – from the surrounding communities. Its population was perhaps 20–30,000.

The visit divides conveniently into public buildings and private houses. Original frescoes and sculptures are still in place, but some are exhibited in Naples' Museo Archeologico (➤ 15).

The Forum is directly up the road from the Porta Marina entrance. Left and right of the entrance to the main square is a temple to Apollo and a basilica housing the chamber of commerce and the courthouse. The Forum was flanked on three sides by two-storey porticoes of Doric and Ionic columns. At the south end, in front of the municipal offices, are plinths for statues of politicians, and a white platform for orators. At the far end is the six-columned Capitolium (shrine) dedicated to Jupiter, Juno and Minerva. In the northeast corner, the porticoed Macellum was the town's main fish, meat and vegetable market.

Via della Abbondanza was a busy thoroughfare leading east from the south end of the Forum; the curved stone paving is rutted by chariot wheels and has raised pedes-

trian crossings. The walls are scratched or daubed in red with ancient graffiti – insults, obscene drawings, advertising and election campaign slogans. To the left, on Vico Lupanare (Brothel Alley) is one of Pompei's 25 registered-brothels, a two-storey building with naughty frescoes.

The Terme Stabiane (Stabian Baths), back on Via della Abbondanza, are built around a porticoed palaestra (gymnasium) with a swimming pool to the left. On the right, beyond the vestibule, men undressed in the *apodyterium*, went from *tepidarium* (warm) to *caldarium* (hot) rooms before cooling off in the *frigidarium*. The women's baths are beyond the furnaces north of the *caldarium*.

The Teatro Grande seated 5,000 spectators to watch the plays of Plautus and Terence, and also gladiators whose *caserma* (barracks) were behind the stage in the large quadriporticus (rectangular building). The smaller, originally roofed, Teatro Piccolo probably staged concerts and poetry recitals.

Of the surviving private houses, three north of the Forum stand out. Casa dei Vettii, belonging to two wealthy ex-slaves, is built around two sides of a columned, peristyle garden. A bold priapic figure in the entrance hall is just the first of many superb wall-paintings. The palatial Casa del Fauno is named after the bronze faun statue in its courtyard, brought to Pompei from Alexandria in the 2nd century BC. It has fine mosaics, a majestic colonnade and a formal garden planted with shrubs common in antiquity. Casa del Poeta Tragico is famous for its threshold mosaic, a fierce chained dog and the timeless inscription 'Cave Canem' (Beware of the Dog).

VILLA DEI MISTERI (➤ 21, TOP TEN)

The bronze faun statue in the Casa del Fauno

SORRENTO

The renowned clifftop resort which enjoyed a heyday in the 19th century remains popular as a base from which to explore the charming Sorrento peninsula and take excursions to Capri (➤ 56), Naples (➤ 26) and along the Amalfi Coast (➤ 66). Sitting on a natural terrace with a sheer drop to the sea and deep ravines on either side, the town is surrounded by lovely gardens, and lemon and orange orchards. Its ancient name is linked by legend to the sirens who tried to lure Ulysses and his sailors on to the treacherous rocks below.

Named after the town's illustrious 16th-century poet Torquato Tasso, whose statue stands at the centre, Piazza Tasso is the gateway to Sorrento's *centro storico* (historic centre). A major monument here is the art nouveau Grand Hotel Vittoria, with ancient marble columns in its gardens left from its predecessor, the villa of Emperor Augustus. Medieval Via Pietà leads to the heart of the old town past the 13th-century Byzantine-style Palazzo Veniero (No 14) and 15th-century Palazzo Correale (No 24), now part of the baroque Santa Maria della Pietà.

Busy Corso Italia has some fashionable boutiques and shops selling the town's famous *limoncello* (lemon liqueur). Across from the much rebuilt campanile of the cathedral, Via Giuliani leads to the Sedile Dominova. This 15th-century arcaded loggia, where the town's nobles held their council, is today a club for card-playing workers. On narrow Via San Cesareo, elegant 17th- and 18th-century buildings rise above the souvenir shops.

Museo Correale di Terranova houses a family collection of Greek and Roman antiquities, Neapolitan painting and European porcelain, glass and clocks.

VESUVIUS (MONTE VESUVIO ➤ 14, TOP TEN)

50B2
Naples Capodichino airport bus; SITA for Amalfi Coast
Circumvesuviana from Naples (Corso Garibaldi)
Hydrofoil from Naples Alilauro ☎ 081 552 7209 Sorrento hydrofoil to Capri and Amalfi Coast ☎ 081 878 1430
Via De Maio 35 ☎ 081 807 4033
Few

Museo Correale di Terranova

Via Correale 48
081 878 1846
Daily 9–2. Closed Tue and public hols
None
Cheap

Above: *in spring, ramblers escape the first crowds to explore the Sorrento coastline along its cliff paths*

Opposite: *Sorrento's harbour is the starting point for cruises along the peninsula or to the island of Capri*

DID YOU KNOW?

Virgil (70–19 BC), whom the Romans considered their greatest poet, lived in Naples while he was writing his *Georgics*. This poetic 'textbook' for farmers about ploughing, orchards, beekeeping and cattle-breeding is best loved for its romantic descriptions of the Italian countryside, gathered on his trips along the Sorrento peninsula and to Capri.

Sorrento to Massa Lubrense

Distance
4km one way

Time
90 minutes one way, 3 hours round trip

Start point
Piazza Tasso, Sorrento
50B2
SITA bus from Amalfi Coast

End point
Largo del Vescovado, Massa Lubrense
50B1
SITA bus

Refreshments
Either in Sorrento or at Massa Lubrense, nothing en route
In Sorrento, The Red Lion, despite its name, has typical local and national dishes at reasonable prices in a pub-like atmosphere. Meals start with a free tomato *bruschetta* and end with a free *limoncello* liqueur.

This is a scenic walk with stunning panoramic views over the Bay of Sorrento and the hills. It is uphill and quite steep for most of the way and a little isolated in some spots. Don't attempt it in intense heat and take plenty of water.

From Piazza Tasso take the Via Casareo, a narrow cobbled street. Towards the end of the road, after about 0.5km, is the Church of SS Annunziata on the left. At the end of the road turn right, then left at the parking sign, which leads to the restaurant zi'ntonio mare. There is a slightly sloping road with a sheer rock face in front. Go along the high-walled path which narrows and becomes a tight passage between two houses, one yellow and one pink. Walk up the steps, go around the railing, and you will find yourself on the busy main road. At the International Camping sign a bit further on the right, turn left up the steep cobbled road and look back to admire the view over the bay.

Among connoisseurs, Massa Lubrense's vineyards are appreciated more for their table grapes than their wine

Negotiate the bends by taking the three paths that act as a shortcut. The road curves left, but go straight over to Via Priora, which takes you across a main road (beware of scooters). Carry on up to a shrine of the Madonna and Child and fork left into a trail in the middle of vineyards and lemon groves. Continue on for another 400m to a crossroads and beyond to join Via Bagnulo. Pass under the arch under the white house, take the first right and go down around two bends to a T-junction. Go left and then first right to Massa Lubrense's Church of Santa Maria Delle Grazie on Largo del Vescavado.

Frequent buses and taxis run back to Sorrento.

Sorrento is very proud of its limoncello *liqueur, but the best is made with Massa Lubrense's lemons*

The Amalfi Coast

The rugged but never forbidding Costiera Amalfitana (Amalfi Coast) is one of Europe's happiest marriages of nature and civilisation. The Lattari Mountains plunge down to the Mediterranean, leaving little space for houses or roads, yet farmers have hewn terraces for vines, and olive and citrus trees join niches of wild rosemary, orchids, cyclamen and honeysuckle. The famous S163 highway somehow winds its way around curves and sudden hairpins. The town of Amalfi (► 67) found a flat shelf at sea level from which to launch its maritime empire, while the houses of Positano (► 18) hang on to the hillside, and Ravello (► 70) withdrew inland, content with the coast's best view. Ruins of mountain lairs and lookout towers attest to the coast's turbulent past, a distant memory in the mellow present.

'No seaman ever passes our shores in his dark vessel till he hears our lips' sweet song and then only, heart filled with the sounds, sails on, a wiser man'

HOMER

Sirens singing from Amalfi Coast in *The Odyssey* (750 BC)

Amalfi

The town's cosmopolitan atmosphere is not something new; Amalfi's central position on the Bay of Salerno marked it out early for a maritime destiny. Starting as a Byzantine protectorate in AD 839, it developed – along with Venice and well before Pisa and Genoa – a commercial empire throughout the Mediterranean.

From the Arabs Amalfi acquired not only architectural models for its duomo (cathedral) and Chiostro del Paradiso (➤ 13), but also the nautical compass to gain a navigational headstart on its rivals. In its 10th- and 11th-century heyday it had trading posts from Tunis to Alexandria and Antioch, and was halted only by the Normans (➤ 8).

After these centuries of commerce, Amalfi offers, on Piazza del Duomo, a delightfully relaxed atmosphere on the terraces of cafés, ice-cream parlours and restaurants looking across to the cathedral's noble stairway. Explore the medieval arcades of Via dei Mercanti (or Ruga Nova) from the foot of the cathedral campanile to the Porta dell'Ospedale. The whitewashed passageway opens out onto little gardens, the Church of Santa Maria Addolorata and the Capo de Ciuccio fountain. On the way are charming antique shops, wine merchants and shops specialising in the locally distilled *limoncello* (lemon liqueur), and potent fruity variations. A popular excursion, just 4km west of town, is to the **Grotta di Smeraldo**, a cave where the waters are as brilliantly emerald green as those of Capri's Grotta Azzurra are sapphire blue.

DUOMO DI AMALFI (➤ 12, TOP TEN)

51C2
Excellent cafés, pizzerias and restaurants around Piazza del Duomo (£–£££)
SITA (from Naples, Sorrento and all coastal resorts)
Travelmar hydrofoil and ferry ☎ 089 873 190
Corso Roma 19–21 ☎ 089 871 107
Few
To beat the high season road traffic, take the hydrofoil or ferry between Positano, Amalfi and Salerno

Grotta di Smeraldo
Statale 163, Conca de Marini
Daily 9–4 Moderate

Amalfi, once a maritime republic, is now a popular resort

DID YOU KNOW?

Playwright Henrik Ibsen worked on *A Doll's House* while staying in Amalfi in 1879 at the 13th-century Franciscan monastery converted into the Luna Convento hotel. A few months later, Richard Wagner was humming themes for his new opera *Parsifal* in the Albergo Capuccini, on the other side of town.

PAESTUM ✪✪✪

The admirably preserved Doric monuments of Paestum are among the finest Greek temples anywhere – including Greece. The temples are at last being liberated from their scaffolding after years of meticulous restoration. Rising majestically from fields by the sea, their honey-coloured stone columns bear witness to Greek colonial prosperity in southern Italy, in particular Poseidonia, as it was known before the Roman conquest in 273 BC. This is perhaps appropriate for a colony founded by traders from Sybaris, whose taste for high living gave rise to the word 'sybarite'.

The temples, dating back to the 5th and 6th centuries BC, stood over the walled city's Roman forum and residential neighbourhoods. Scholars dispute the temples' modern names. At the southern end of the ancient city, the building with a nine-columned façade, mistakenly known as the Basilica, was more likely to have been a temple of Hera, the city's patron goddess. The interior's division in two by a central row of columns suggests worship of a second deity, perhaps Zeus. It was built around 530 BC, about 100 years before its taller neighbour, Tempio di Nettuno (➤ 20). At the north end of the site, the discovery of Christian tombs suggests that the hexastyle (six-column façade) Temple of Athena, also mistakenly attributed to Ceres, was used as a church in the Middle Ages.

The **Museo Archeologico** exhibits Paestum's sculpture, ceramics and other works of art, most notably the Tomba del Tuffatore (Diver's Tomb) from the 5th century BC, a rare example of Greek mural painting.

51D1
Via Magna Grecia
Daily 9 to one hour before sunset
Nettuno (£–££), Via Principe di Piemonte ☎ 082 881 1028
From Salerno, Piazza Concordia
Paestum on Salerno–Reggio di Calabria line
☎ 082 881 1016
Few
Expensive (moderate if combining museum and temples)
Guided tours; occasional lectures

Museo Archeologico
☎ 082 881 1023
Daily 9–6:30. Closed first and third Mon in the month

Paestum's Basilica may have been a dual temple for Hera, the city's patron goddess, and her husband, Zeus

POSITANO (➤ 18, TOP TEN)

Montepertuso Walks

For an exhilarating excursion away from the resort of Positano, take a bus to the hillside village of Montepertuso, an idyllic start for a country walk.

Montepertuso is a peaceful little community perched 365m above Positano, taking its name from a crag above the village 'pierced' (*pertuso*) by a gaping hole. Houses with charming terraced gardens cluster around the small white-towered Church of Santa Maria delle Grazie. You may just be content to wind your way from the main piazza, passing to the right of the church downhill through olive groves back to Positano, an easy and very pretty one-hour walk.

For a longer, but not at all strenuous walk, also starting out from the Montepertuso piazza, make your way east for just 45 minutes to the delightful flowery little village of Nocelle, 80m higher up the mountainside. It lies on the other side of a ravine spanned by a fine arched footbridge. The road from Nocelle's Church of Santa Croce back to Positano is then a pleasant 90-minute walk down a lightly wooded hillside fragrant with rosemary.

A more ambitious ramble is rewarded with spectacular panoramas of cypress and pine groves up in the Lattari Mountains. This challenging but not arduous 90-minute hike takes you uphill behind Montepertuso to the Caserma Forestale, forest barracks built of solid stone 770m above sea level. Another 20-minutes' walk beyond Caserma are beautiful views back down the hillside to Nocelle and Positano, and out to sea to the islands of Capri and Ischia. The one-hour walk back zigzags easily down to the Montepertuso bus stop.

Time
Take a whole day to wander

Start/end point
Positano
51C2

SITA bus from Bar Internazionale stop, Positano

Positano 089 875 067

Lunch
Cafés (£) and restaurants (£–£££) in both Montepertuso and Nocelle

Wild rosemary adds charm and fragrance to the mountain walks down to Positano

The garden at Villa Cimbrone with its Moorish tea-room

- 51C2
- Cafés, restaurants (£–££) around Piazza Duomo
- SITA bus once daily from Naples, hourly from Amalfi 6AM–9PM
- Piazza Duomo 089 857 096
- Few
- Summer Wagner Festival (➤ 85)

Villa Cimbrone

- Via Santa Chiara
- May–Sep 9–8PM; Oct–Apr 9AM to sunset
- Few Moderate

Ceramic vases in Ravello

RAVELLO ✪✪

About 350m above Amalfi, the sumptuous villas of the town perch with aloof gentility among umbrella pines and lofty cypresses on a ridge flanked by the Dragone and Reginna valleys. Ancient Romans fled here from invading Visigoths and Huns; today, holidaymakers come to escape the crowds down on the coast. Strolling around the magnificent gardens here and looking out to sea, along the tree-shaded cobbled lanes, or just sitting on the medieval Piazza Duomo, it is very easy to forget there is any other place on earth.

The medieval connection with the Duchy of Amalfi, and the lucrative role Ravello played in trade with Sicily, becomes clear both in the town's churches and its older villas, each showing the influence of Byzantine and Arab architectural styles – most notably the lovely Villa Rufolo (➤ 22), opposite the Duomo. The 11th-century cathedral has undergone heavy-handed baroque transformations, but its 13th-century campanile, with its handsome twin-mullioned windows, has the characteristic intertwining arches of Arab architecture. Inside the church, the richly decorated marble pulpit, borne aloft by six lions, captures the opulent style of the eastern Mediterranean. North of the Duomo, these elements reappear in the multiple domed 12th-century Church of San Giovanni del Toro. Inside, Aldano da Termoli's pulpit (1200) has blue Persian stone basins.

At the southern end of Ravello, the grandiose **Villa Cimbrone** was built in the 18th century and ingeniously incorporates ancient columns and medieval sculpture from the town's various churches and palazzi. Its splendid garden with a belvedere at the far edge of the Ravello ridge was landscaped by Lord Grimthorpe, designer of the clock-mechanism for London's Big Ben.

SALERNO

The Allied army landings here in September 1943 made this key industrial port the capital of liberated Italy for a few proud months. But war – and earthquake – have destroyed much of what was once an important university town, famous for its medical school since the Middle Ages.

Today its historic centre has been reduced to a few narrow lanes around the Via Portacatena, which extends through the 8th-century Arco di Arechi to the picturesque Via dei Mercanti. There is a fine view of the old town from the Castello di Arechi, which houses a museum of Salerno's history.

51C2
SITA from Naples and Amalfi Coast resorts
Hydrofoil from Positano, Amalfi (Travelmar ☎ 089 873 190)
Via Roma 258 ☎ 089 224 744
Few
Paestum (➤ 68)

Since World War II, the old university town of Salerno has become a thoroughly modern city

Salerno's magnificent cathedral was built in 1076 by the town's Norman conqueror, Robert Guiscard. It underwent extensive transformations in the 17th and 18th centuries, but with the rare harmonious incorporation of existing architectural elements – ancient Greek, Byzantine, Arab and Romanesque. Set in a neo-classical façade, the portal at the top of its stairway, Porta dei Leoni, is adorned with Romanesque sculpted lions and an atrium with intertwining Arab arches supported by Greek columns from Paestum's temples. The monumental black doors were fashioned in Constantinople and set between classical Byzantine columns. But nothing is more lavish than the polychrome marble for the baroque crypt, rebuilt in the 17th century to house the relics of the Apostle Matthew. Over the double altar are two bronze statues of the saint (1622). The next door museum contains an early medieval altar-front, embellished with 54 superb ivory panels.

Positano to Salerno

Distance
70–80km

Time
Take a whole day

Start point
Positano
✚ 51C2

End point
Salerno
✚ 51C2

Lunch
Le Arcate (£–££)
✉ Via G Di Benedetto 4, Atrani
☎ 089 871 367

This is the famous Amalfi Drive along the coast road, taking in the 'Big Three' resorts: Positano (➤ 18), Amalfi (➤ 67) and Ravello (➤ 70). But on the way, it also offers a glimpse of smaller fishing villages and market towns like Praiano, Atrani and Vietro, and briefly leaves the coastal highway after Amalfi for an incursion inland to look at the Lattari Mountains. It is particularly worthwhile going on to Salerno (➤ 71) if you are planning an excursion down to Paestum (➤ 68).

From Positano, turn east and stay on the S163 until just after Amalfi, at Atrani. On this road more than most, keep well to the right and do not hesitate to use the horn on blind curves.

Praiano's fishermen's houses are scattered across the ridge of Monte Sant'Angelo, and Marina di Praia is a charming little beach. Just before Conca dei Marini are signposts for the translucent green waters of the Grotta di Smeraldo (➤ 67). Atrani is one of the coast's prettiest little towns, particularly on Piazza Umberto I.

The campanile of the 13th-century Church of the Maddalena dominates the skyline of Atrani

About 1km after Atrani, turn left at the Ravello exit. From the tunnel passing under Ravello, go left on the highway signposted Valico Chiunzi. Continue to the crossroads on the crest of the Lattari Mountain ridge, then turn right to take the highway back to the coast, signposted Maiori.

This detour loops around the Tramonti plain, with some impressive rugged mountain views along the way. At this altitude, orange and lemon trees are replaced by vineyards and vegetable gardens with aubergines, tomatoes and bell-peppers.

At Maiori, turn left on to the S163 to continue via Vietri to Salerno.

Vietri is famous for its majolica ceramics, both for domestic and monumental use. Notice the dome on the parish church of San Giovanni Batista.

Where To...

Above: *rows of cheeses*
Right: a *Spaccanapoli toy-seller demonstrates local priorities: two footballs for every Mickey Mouse*

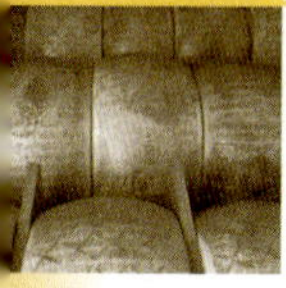

Naples

Prices
£ = under 15 Euros
££ = 15–33 Euros
£££ = over 33 Euros

Meals
Neapolitans take their breakfast (*prima colazione*) standing at the counter, a cappuccino or a kick-start *ristretto*, a thimbleful of concentrated espresso, and a crisp *sfogliatella* or softer *cornetto* (croissant) with jam or sweet ricotta filling. The café breakfast will always be better – and cheaper – than at a hotel. Lunch (*pranzo*) begins after noon, dinner (*cena*) from 8PM, generally later in Naples, Capri, Positano and Amalfi than in the smaller towns.

Bellini (£–££)
In the student district with shady terrace. Popular up-market pizzeria and good all-round trattoria. Try house Pizza Bellini (mozzarella, ham and mushrooms), *linguine con frutti di mare* (seafood pasta) or fine grilled fish.
Via Costantinopoli 74 081 459 774 Closed Sun, week in mid-Aug R1, R4

Brandi (£–££)
Having created the flagship Pizza Margherita in 1889 (► 36), this venerable pizzeria still attracts crowds. Try, too, *pizza all'ortolana* (garden vegetables) or *pescatora* (seafood). Delicious rum baba.
Salita Sant'Anna di Palazzo 1 (behind Piazza Trieste e Trento) 081 123 4567 Closed three days in mid-Aug R2, R3

La Cantinella (£££)
Elegant address near big Santa Lucia hotels. Exquisite service, fresh seafood and exceptional wine cellar attract Naples' high society. Seafood pasta (*pappardelle agli scampi* and *tagliatelle Santa Lucia*) and monkfish in seafood sauce (*rana pescatrice*) are house specialities. Pastry chef does wonders with oranges and lemons.
Via Cuma 42 081 764 8684 Closed Sun, mid-Aug R3

Caruso (£££)
Romantic views over the Bay of Naples and Castel dell' Ovo is the major appeal of this celebrated roof garden restaurant at the top of the Vesuvio hotel. Try maestro's *bucatini Enrico Caruso*.
Grande Albergo Vesuvio, Via Partenope 45 081 764 0520 Daily R3

La Chiacchierata (££)
Family trattoria near Piazza del Plebiscito, with Mamma Anna cooking and checking everybody is happy. Robust cuisine, lusty vegetable soups. Daily change of menu, so let Anna choose for you. *Chiacchierata* means 'chat'.
Piazzetta Matilde Serao 37 081 411 465 Mon–Thu lunch only, Fri, Sat lunch and dinner. Closed Sun and Aug R2, R3

Al Cinquantatre (££)
Long-established trattoria in *centro storico* with pleasant terrace. Traditional Neapolitan cooking attracts both neighbourhood regulars and discerning foreign clientele. Big choice of *antipasti*; savoury speciality is *minestra maritata* soup, and lasagne is first rate.
Piazza Dante 53 081 549 9372 Closed Tue R1, R4

Ciro a Santa Brigida (££–£££)
Run by the Pace family for over 100 years. Highest quality; subtle *antipasti*, old-fashioned *o pignatiello de vavella* (shellfish soup), seafood or vegetable pasta, and *pizza d'oro*, with whole cherry tomatoes.
Via Santa Brigida 71, near Galleria Umberto I 081 552 4072 Closed Sun R2

Giuseppone a Mare (££–£££)
One of Naples' top seafood restaurants with a grand bay view. Fresh fish, *tagliatelle al*

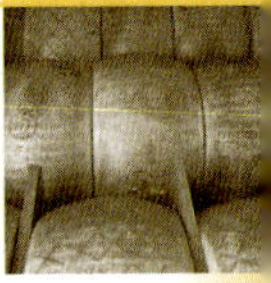

tartufo e asparagi (truffles and asparagus), and *linguine al nero* (in squid ink). Good wines, rich choice of desserts.
Via Ferdinando Russo 13, Capo Posillipo 081 123 4567 Closed Sun, Aug, Christmas C21

Masaniello (££)
In the stableblock of an old *palazzo* in *centro storico*, you can expect to find traditional Neapolitan dishes and great pizzas – especially with *rucola* (rocket) or *salsiccie* (sausage).
Via Donnalbina 28 (behind Santa Maria La Nova church) 081 552 8863 Closed Sun eve, few days Aug R1

Di Matteo (£)
Di Matteo was Spacca-napoli's best-loved pizzeria long before President Bill Clinton visited in 1994, but it's even more crowded now. Expect to have to queue, but it's worth the wait. The Margherita is the purists' choice, commonly eaten Neapolitan-style *a libretto* (folded in two).
Via Tribunali 94 081 455 262 Closed Sun, two weeks in Aug Piazza Cavour

Mimi Alla Ferrovia (££–£££)
Grand family institution with a reputation for fine food, sufficient to make people miss trains. Simplicity and finesse combine in *pasta e fagioli* (noodles and beans) and famous *linguine al Mimi* (scampi, shrimp, scallops) and plain fennel salad.
Via Alfonsa d'Aragona 21 081 553 8525 Closed Sun, week in mid-Aug Piazza Garibaldi

Osteria Castello (£)
A modest family trattoria in fashionable Chiaia serving fine *bucatini all'amatriciana* (pasta with ham and red bell-peppers), pepper steaks and good home-made desserts.
Via Santa Teresa a Chiaia 38 081 400 486 Closed Sun, Aug R3

La Sacrestia (£££)
Overlooking the bay from Posillipo, this is one of Naples' most prestigious restaurants. The menu includes exquisite aubergine (eggplant) ravioli, delicate *fagottini* (pasta rolls with chives, ricotta and spinach), fresh fish, and an excellent wine list.
Via Orazio 116 081 761 1051 Closed Sun dinner, Mon lunch C21

Taverna dell'Arte (££)
With tasteful and romantic décor, this fine old trattoria in the *centro storico* serves typical Neapolitan dishes: *minestra maritata* soup, stuffed pork, a great variety of vegetables and good local wines.
Rampa San Giovanni Maggiore 1a 081 552 7558 Dinner only. Closed Sun R2

Around Naples

Casertavecchia
La Castellana (££)
A pretty garden restaurant in this medieval hilltop village. Try the home-made pasta and savoury wild mushroom dishes.
Via Torre 4, Casertavecchia (10km from Caserta's royal palace) 082 337 1230 Closed Thu Caserta–Reggia (taxi)

Menu as Art
In this land of painters, the menu is often displayed on a trattoria counter as an appetising still-life: *antipasti* (starters) such as *peperoni*, marinated and grilled red, green and yellow bell-peppers, *calamari* (baby squid); *primo piatto* (first course) pasta, risotto or pizza are back in the kitchen; *secondo piatto* meat or fish are kept fresh on crushed ice; and near by you will see mozzarella cheese, plates of fresh *fichi* (figs) and *uva* (grapes).

Bay of Naples

A Real Bill
Asking for the bill, '*Il conto, per favore*', gives you the right to ask for something more legible than a sum scribbled on a scrap of paper. Ask for a *ricevuta* and you will be given the legally required receipt bearing the restaurant's printed name and clearly itemised bill along with a 15 per cent service charge, and often a small cover charge (*pane e coperto*). Any additional tip is at your own discretion.

Bacoli

Da Giona (££)
Beachfront seafood trattoria on the quiet cape west of Bacoli. Worth seeking out for the fish soup, pasta and *risotto frutti di mare* (seafood), and fresh fish; which are very good value for this resort area.
Via Dragonara 6, Capo Miseno 081 523 4659 Closed Thu

Baia

L'Altro Cucchiaro (£££)
One of Italy's finest seafood restaurants overlooking Baia's pretty harbour. Follow fresh *fritturine* (fried whitebait) with gnocchi or spaghettini in seafood sauce, or oven-baked *rana pescatrice* (monkfish). Terrific desserts.
Via Lucullo 13, Baia Porto 081 868 7196 Dinner only. Closed Sun, Mon, Aug

Capri

Aurora (££)
In the heart of Capri old town. Traditional cooking: grilled vegetables, seafood pasta, the fresh catch of the day, and great pizza.
Via Fuorlavado 18 081 837 0181 Closed Jan–Mar

Quisi (£££)
Legendary hotel restaurant at legendary prices, but still providing the ultimate in luxury and refinement. Specialities include *fiorilli di zucca ripieni* (stuffed marrow), fish pâté, pasta with scampi and cherry tomatoes, *quaglia con castagne* (quail with chestnuts and foie gras).
Grand Hotel Quisisana, Via Camerelle 2 081 837 0788 Dinner only, Easter to Nov

La Savardina da Edoardo (£–££)
There is a lovely walk from Capri Town to this charming trattoria in a citrus garden. Try linguine in herbs, cherry tomatoes, garlic and fresh anchovy; ravioli with *caciotta* cheese; or rabbit (*coniglio*) in white wine.
Via Lo Capo 081 837 6300 Closed Nov–Feb

Pozzuoli

Michelemmá (££–£££)
Set in a lemon grove with live evening music. Specialities are shellfish linguine or gnocchi, grilled fish, and good seafood pizzas, with crêpes or homebaked pies for dessert.
Via Carlo Rosini 27 081 526 2749 Closed Mon in summer; Tue, Wed in winter

Sant'Agata

Don Alfonso (£££)
One of southern Italy's most celebrated restaurants is in this pretty pink villa. The house specialities include *cipolla novella farcita* (spring onions stuffed with shrimp and bacon), *penne alle calamarette* (pasta with baby squid), *capretto lucano* (goat kid), and chocolate and wild cherry soufflé.
Piazza Sant'Agata 081 878 0026 Closed Mon; Tue in winter

Sorrento

O Parrucchiano (££)
Nicknamed La Favorita, this Sorrento institution does a roaring trade all year round. The recommended dishes here are cannelloni, gnocchi and fish simply grilled with a little lemon.
Corso Italia 71 081 878 1321 Closed Wed in winter

The Amalfi Coast

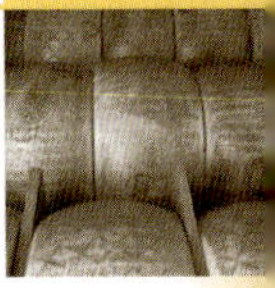

Amalfi

Da Gemma (£££)

Over 120 years old and still going strong in this elegant neighbourhood. Try the wonderfully rich fish soup, the *linguine all'aragosta* (spiny lobster), or fresh fish, grilled or in white wine sauce. Da Gemma also has a fine wine cellar.

Via Fra'Gerardo Sasso 10, near Piazza del Duomo 089 871 1345 Closed Wed in winter, and 15 Jan–15 Feb

Da Maria (££)

A delightfully friendly, family trattoria serving traditional regional dishes, good fresh vegetables, varied *antipasti*, seafood pasta, the best of the local wines, and great pizza.

Via Lorenzo di Amalfi 14, just off Piazza del Duomo 089 871 880 Closed Mon

Atrani

Le Arcate (£–££)

Come here for some excellent simple local dishes in a charming setting near the harbour in Atrani. There's good fresh seafood and friendly family service.

Via G Di Benedetto 4 089 871 367 Closed Mon off-season, and 15 Jan–15 Feb

Paestum

Nettuno (£–££)

With its fine terrace view of Paestum's most beautiful temples (► 68), this smart trattoria serves honest regional cuisine, good pasta and risotto with excellent locally sourced seafood sauces.

Via Principe di Piemonte 082 881 1028 Closed Mon off-season

Positano

La Buca di Bacco (££–£££)

Beachfront trattoria popular with families and yachters for snacks and sumptuous gourmet cuisine, fresh seafood and savoury pastas.

Via Rampa Teglia 8 089 875 699 Closed Nov–Mar

La Sponda (£££)

Positano's finest food is exquisitely served in this luxurious but friendly family-run hotel. The cuisine is traditional but delicate and imaginative: seafood pasta and risotto, mixed grill of fresh fish and oven-baked local *pezzogna* fish. Fantastic rum baba or *torta di mandorla* (almond tart).

Le Sirenuse Hotel, Via Cristoforo Colombo 30 081 123 4567 Daily all year

Ravello

Cumpa Cosimo (£–££)

Very popular with local residents as well as foreign celebrities (there are photos of Humphrey Bogart and Jackie Kennedy) for the unfailing quality of the pasta and seafood dishes, served in an agreeable atmosphere.

Via Roma 42 089 857 156 Closed Mon off-season

Palumbo (£££)

Palatial dining in the medieval Palazzo Confalone, now a luxury hotel, with superb terrace view of Amalfi Coast. Try *insalata di seppioline* (baby squid with walnuts and celery), ravioli with mint (*menta*), *spigola all'arancia* (sea bass in orange sauce), and fine Ravello wines.

Via San Giovanni del Toro 16 089 857 244 Closed 6 Jan–15 Mar

Soft Drinks

Citrus orchards in Naples' monastery gardens and the surrounding country ensure you always get the freshest of freshly squeezed orange juice (*spremuta di arancia*). Other café and bar favourites are freshly squeezed grapefruit (*spremuta di pompelmo*), and bottled juice (*succo di frutta*) of apricot (*albicocca*), peach (*pesca*) and pear (*pera*). Iced coffee (*granita di caffé*) is usually coffee syrup poured over crushed ice. A milkshake is *frullato di latte*.

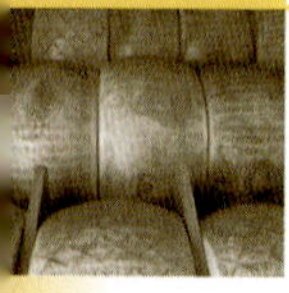

Naples

Prices
All hotels accept major credit cards, unless stated otherwise. The price ranges used here are for a twin room.
£ = under 80 Euros
££ = 80–105 Euros
£££ = over 105 Euros

Booking
Good accommodation in Naples is not plentiful, so you need to book well in advance. Advance booking by credit card is increasingly accepted. For the Naples area (which includes Capri, Ischia, Pompei, Sorrento and the Campi Flegrei), Naples Tourist Office (➤ 88) provides a complete official listing *(Napoli e Provincia: Annuario Alberghi)* detailing amenities and prices for the year of publication. Similar information for the Amalfi Coast is available through each individual resort's tourist office.

Albergo Sansevero (£)
The more recent of two charming boarding houses, modest but clean and comfortable, in an 18th-century palazzo. Of eight rooms, all with bath, two overlook pretty Piazza Bellini.
✉ Via Santa Maria di Costantinopoli 101 ☎ 081 210 907; fax 081 211 698 🚌 R1, R4

Canada (£–££)
Overlooking Mergellina harbour, very simple but clean, air-conditioned accommodation; 12 rooms with tiny baths. Convenient for hydrofoil to Capri.
✉ Via Mergellina 43 ☎ 081 680 952; fax 081 651 594 🚆 Mergellina

Cavour (££)
Modern, well-run, family hotel by Stazione Centrale. Rooms (96) are spacious, simply furnished, air-conditioned, some with balcony, but ask for double-glazing (*con doppi vetri*). Good restaurant.
✉ Piazza Garibaldi 32 ☎ 081 283 122; fax 081 287 488 🚆 Piazza Garibaldi

Excelsior (£££)
A grand hotel from the *belle époque*; magnificent roof-garden view of Castel dell'Ovo.
✉ Via Partenope 44 ☎ 081 764 0111; fax 081 764 4661 🚌 3

Pinto Storey (££)
Fashionable location behind Villa Pignatelli. Rooms (25) tastefully furnished; impeccable bedlinen and bathrooms; friendly service. Lovely breakfast room.
✉ Via Giuseppe Martucci 72 ☎ 081 681 260; fax 081 667 536 🚌 R3

Rex (££)
Just off Santa Lucia seafront, in an old palazzo restored from war damage but with original ceiling paintings and art nouveau decor. Bright, colourful rooms (40), double-glazed and air-conditioned.
✉ Via Palepoli 12 ☎ 081 764 9389; fax 081 764 9227 🚌 R3

Santa Lucia (£££)
Renovated neo-classical seafront hotel. Elegant, spacious and comfortable rooms (102). Breakfast buffet a major attraction.
✉ Via Partenope 46 ☎ 081 764 0666; fax 081 764 8580 🚌 R3

Soggiorno Sansevero (£)
Under same management as Albergo, this boarding house occupies part of the legendary Sansevero princes' palazzo. Private baths in four of six clean, comfortable rooms. Breakfast in famous Scaturchio Café included.
✉ Piazza San Domenico Maggiore 9 ☎ 081 551 5949 🚌 R1

Vesuvio (£££)
Ultimate luxury hotel. Opulently furnished rooms with tapestries; bay view. Enrico Caruso left his name on the most luxurious suite, the rooftop restaurant, and his favourite pasta.
✉ Via Partenope ☎ 081 764 0044; fax 081 764 4483 🚌 R3

Villa Capodimonte (£££)
A modern but stylishly decorated establishment in a tranquil hillside location near Capodimonte Museum and park. Terrace restaurant and tennis court.
✉ Via Moiariello 66 ☎ 081 459 000; fax 081 299 344 🚌 110

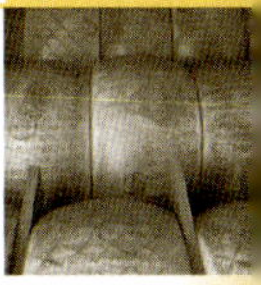

Bay of Naples & the Amalfi Coast

Capri

Quisisana (£££)
Originally a high-class 19th-century sanatorium, now one of the world's best-known luxury hotels. Facilities include tennis, gym, indoor and outdoor swimming pools and two restaurants.
Via Camerelle 2 081 837 0788; fax 081 837 6080 Closed Nov–Mar

Villa Krupp (££)
Simple comfort in 12 rooms – originally home to Russian writer Maxim Gorky. Splendid view of Faraglioni rocks and Marina Piccola.
Via Matteotti 12, near Parco Augusto 081 837 0362; fax 081 837 6489 Closed Jan

Ischia

Villa Angelica (£–££)
Charming family villa in a quiet street on north coast. Garden swimming pool fed by a hot spring.
Via IV Novembre 28, Lacco Ameno 081 994 524; fax 081 980 184 Nov–15 April

Sorrento

Excelsior Vittoria (£££)
Enduring monument and home of stars from Caruso to Pavarotti. Marble bathrooms, romantic view of Capri. Swimming pool, enchanting gardens.
Piazza Tasso 34 081 807 1044

Amalfi Coast

Amalfi

La Bussola (£–££)
Pleasant family hotel nicely situated on harbour promenade. Neat, functional rooms, friendly service.
Lungomare dei Cavalieri 1/e 089 871 533; fax 089 871 369

Cappuccini Convento (£££)
Converted from a medieval monastery in 1821, high above Amalfi town, there's a real but sober comfort in the monks' cells. Private beach.
Via Annunziatella 46
089 871 877; fax 089 871 886

Luna Convento (£££)
Seafront hotel which began life as a Franciscan monastery in 1222. Superbly furnished with majolica-tiled interiors. The 15 rooms were originally monks' cells. Ibsen wrote *A Doll's House* here.
Via Comite 19 089 871 002; fax 089 871 333

Positano

Casa Albertina (££)
Cordially run family hotel in classic Mediterranean house. Air-conditioned rooms are small but cosy. Good home cooking.
Via della Tavolozza 3
089 875 143; fax 089 811 540

Sirenuse (£££)
One of southern Italy's finest hotels, run by an aristocratic family in their 18th-century villa. Rooms are furnished with exquisite taste in traditional Mediterranean style. First-class restaurant and the coast's best swimming pool.
Via Cristoforo Colombo 30
089 875 066; fax 089 811 798

Ravello

Palumbo (£££)
Opulent hotel occupying medieval Palazzo Confalone, which Wagner made his home while working on *Parsifal*. The spacious rooms have views of the gardens and orange groves.
Via San Giovanni del Toro 16 081 123 4567

Agriturismo
Self-catering in farmhouse accommodation is a good and cheaper way of getting to know the countryside around Naples and the country behind the Amalfi Coast. Some are purpose built for tourists but located on a working farm. You will need a car to get around – and maybe better Italian than is necessary in town. Details from local tourist offices or regional listings from Agriturist Campania Corso Lucci, 137, Naples 081 285 243. National office: Agriturist Corso Vittorio Emanuele 101, 00186 Rome 06 685 2342.

Naples

Christmas Figurines
The Neapolitan art of modelling miniature figures for *presepe* (Christmas mangers) began 600 years ago, inspired by Francis of Assisi's live re-enactment of the scene at Greccio in 1223. Since its baroque heyday, the tradition thrives all year round in workshops around Via San Gregorio Armeno. With meticulous attention to detail, artisans add to symbolic religious figures – Holy Family, angels, shepherds, Three Kings – characters from the streets of Naples, along with filmstars, footballers and politicians. See them at work at Certosa di San Martino (► 30), although the most famous workshop is:

Ferrigno
✉ Via San Gregorio Armeno 8
☎ 081 552 3148

Antiques & Books

Bowinkel
Wonderful collection of Naples prints, photographs, bronzes, fans, costumes.
✉ Piazza dei Martiri 24 ☎ 081 764 4344 🚌 R2, R3

Feltrinelli
Naples' best all-round bookshop with range of English-language literature.
✉ Via San Tommaso d'Aquino 70/76 ☎ 081 552 1436 🚌 R2, R3

Fiera Antiquaria
Antiques fair in municipal park two weekends a month.
✉ Viale Anton Dohrn, Villa Comunale ☎ 081 761 2541 🚌 R2, R3

Guida
Matchless selection of second-hand and rare books.
✉ Via Port'Alba 20/23 ☎ 081 446 377 🚌 R1, R4

Pignasecca Flea Market
Occasional antiques turn up among the usual bric-à-brac.
✉ Off Piazza Caritá 🚌 R1, R4

Treves
Good selection of Italian and international novels.
✉ Via Toledo 249/250 ☎ 081 415 211 🚌 R1, R4

Fashion & Jewellery

Aldo Tramontana
Renowned for its *haute couture* leather goods.
✉ Via Chiaia 149 ☎ 081 414 758 🚌 R2, R3

Brinkmann
Meticulously handcrafted jewellery.
✉ Piazza Municipio 21 ☎ 081 552 0555 🚌 R2, R3

Caso
Highly reputed for its antique jewels, vintage watches and delicate coralware.
✉ Piazza San Domenico Maggiore 16 ☎ 081 741 4672

Marinella
Made-to-measure ties for celebrities and heads of state including Bill Clinton.
✉ Riviera di Chiaia 287 ☎ 081 245 1182 🚌 R2, R3

Pistola
Remains king of Naples glovemakers, working in finest lamb- and kid-skin.
✉ Via Santa Caterina a Chiaia 12 ☎ 081 422 058 🚌 R2, R3

Gourmet Foods

Gastronomia LUISE
Sophisticated delicatessen for both Neapolitan and French specialities.
✉ Via Toledo 266/269 ☎ 081 407 852 🚌 R1, R4

Scaturchio
Historic pastry shop famous for its *sfogliatelle* and house specialities; *zeffiro all'arancia* (orange delicacy), and chocolate and rum *ministeriale*.
✉ Piazza San Domenico Maggiore 19 ☎ 081 551 6944

Supermarkets

Mida 3
Conveniently located near Stazione Centrale to buy a picnic for an excursion.
✉ Via Maddalena 40 ☎ 081 281 254 🚇 Piazza Garibaldi

SI
One of a few supermarkets in the *centro storico*.
✉ Via San Tommaso d'Aquino ☎ 081 551 3725 🚌 R2, R3

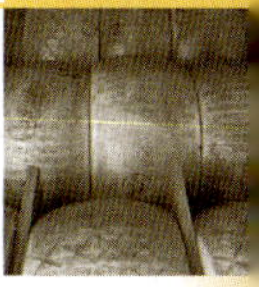

Bay of Naples & the Amalfi Coast

Antiques

Siniscalco-Gori
Gallery of classical antiques and paintings, mostly 19th and early 20th century.
✉ Via Camerelle 89, Capri
☎ 081 837 6798

Crafts & Ceramics

Cartiera Amatruda
From Italy's oldest paper-mills, the Amatruda family has handcrafted paper goods for over 800 years. Its notebooks seem almost too good to actually use.
✉ Via Fiume, Amalfi ☎ 089 871 315

Ceramiche Solimene
Using time-honoured methods for handcrafted tableware, ceramicists will paint customer's personally chosen designs.
✉ Via XXV Luglio 15, Vietri
☎ 089 210 048

Di Maia
Acknowledged master of *intarsia* (inlaid wood) tables, trays and other household wares, based on the patterns of ancient Sorrento mosaics.
✉ Via degli Archi 16, Sorrento
☎ 081 878 4656

Mennella
Traditional island craftwork, pottery and majolica tiling.
✉ Casamicciola Terme, Via San Girardi 47, Ischia ☎ 081 994 442

Rosbenia
Bedlinen, tablecloth and napkins – all hand-embroidered in finest linen and lace. The place to come for wedding gifts.
✉ Piazza Laura 34, Sorrento
☎ 081 877 2341

Fashion

Canfora
Famous for handmade, classic shoes, stylish and not exorbitant.
✉ Via Camerelle 3, Capri
☎ 081 837 0487

Costanzo Avitabile
Positano's famous stylish sandals are made to measure while you wait.
✉ Piazza Amerigo Vespucci 1–5, Positano ☎ 089 875 366

Maria Lampo
For men, women and children, smart summer slacks, shorts and beachwear, made from Positano's traditional fabrics.
✉ Via Pasitea 12–4, Positano
☎ 089 875 021

Perfume & Jewellery

La Campanina
An Aladdin's cave of elegantly mounted diamonds, sapphires and other stones, but also fine coral bracelets and necklaces.
✉ Via Vittorio Emanuele 18, Capri ☎ 081 837 0643

Carthusia
This is the place to buy Capri's unique perfumes, not available outside the island.
✉ Via Camerelle 10, Capri
☎ 081 837 0529

Wines

Enoteca D'Ambra
Wine-tasting and sales of island produce from Ischia's century-old family-run vineyards.
✉ Porto, Via Porto 24, Ischia
☎ 081 991 046

Limoncello
Amalfi, Capri and Sorrento all lay claim to producing the finest *limoncello* liqueur. When prepared properly, ice cold but not on ice, the best is slightly sour, and never too sweet. Very often a fancy bottle, however attractive to recycle as a carafe, betrays inferior quality. Decide for yourself:
Antichi Sapori d'Amalfi
✉ Via Supportico Ferrari 4, Amalfi
☎ 089 872 303
Limoncello di Capri
✉ Via Roma 79, Capri
☎ 081 837 5561
Piemme
✉ Corso Italia 161/163, Sorrento
☎ 081 807 297

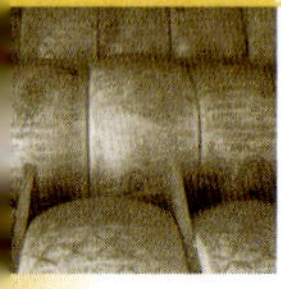

Naples

Little Horrors
Most children love being terrified (a little). This is amply catered for by the baroque side of Naples, and the region's natural disasters. In Cappella Sansevero (➤ 28), children are delighted by anatomically precise entrails inside two life-size skeletons. At the Capodimonte Museum (➤ 16–17), squeals of joy greet Artemisia Gentileschi's excruciating portrayal of Judith beheading Holofernes. No visit to Pompei (➤ 60–1) is complete without seeing ancient corpses petrified by Vesuvius. Some kids even like the stinky sulphurous fumaroles spouting at Campi Flegrei's Solfatara (➤ 54). And for the ultimate scare, order (in secret) a plate of *spaghetti al nero* (in squid ink sauce).

Amusement Park

Edenlandia
This huge funfair is out at Mostra d'Oltremare trade fairgrounds to the west of Mergellina.
✉ Viale Kennedy ☎ 081 239 1182 🚆 Ferrovia Cumana (Montesanto) to Edenlandia

Food
How can you go wrong in a place that makes the best pizza in the world? In the same restaurant that serves something dauntingly delicate to their parents, maybe fish with bones, kids can have their favourite *quattro staggione* or Margherita, or discover a pocket *calzone* (actually 'trousers') pizza they can eat with both fists. Or easy-to-eat macaroni in all shapes and sizes – penne, rigatoni, fusilli, farfalle. Do they know architects are employed to design these things? For breakfast, crispy sweet *sfogliatelle* make a welcome change from cornflakes. And then there's the ice-cream… In Naples you will find the origins of much of todays's most popular foods. It will be easy to take them out once they know this!

Ice-cream

Bilancione
There are usually long seafront queues for the city's most popular ice-cream parlour. The hazelnut (*nocciola*) has won a Golden Cone (*Cona d'Oro*) in the world ice-cream champion-ships. The exquisite fresh fruit flavours change with the seasons.
✉ Via Posillipo 238 ☎ 081 769 1923

Otranto
For the creamiest concoctions in 30 ever-changing flavours near Certosa di San Martino.
✉ Via Michele Kerbaker 43
☎ 081 578 0538

La Scimmia
A pioneer on Naples' *gelati* scene (for over 60 years), La Scimmia made its name with classic banana, but they also do great *crema torrone* (nougat) and pistachio.
✉ Piazza Caritá 4 (off Via Toledo) ☎ 081 552 0272

Museums and Castles
Even if you cannot coax them inside the Capodimonte museum (➤ 16–17), children enjoy the pretty palace gardens, so take a picnic – and a football which, despite signposts to the contrary, is a favourite pastime there. A big attraction at the Certosa di San Martino (➤ 30) is the collection of *presepe* (Christmas mangers). And there is always the formidable medieval Castel Sant'Elmo (➤ 29) next door. Kids like Castel Nuovo (➤ 29) and its stories – more horror – of torture and crocodiles in the dungeons. An attraction at the Museo Archeologico (➤ 15) is the huge scale model of Pompei, useful before your trip there.

Toys and Dolls

Ospedale delle Bambole
This tiny doll's hospital in the heart of Spaccanapoli is one of the city's most enchanting shops.
✉ Via San Biagio dei Librai 81
☎ 081 203 067

Bay of Naples & the Amalfi Coast

Beaches

Ischia's north coast (➤ 59) offers the best sandy beaches for family swimming and watersports. A popular beach on the south coast is the volcanic Spiaggia del Maronti. Positano (➤ 18) has several beaches and coves, fairly close to the harbour. La Porta has the added attraction of Stone Age cave dwellings to explore. To reach Capri's best beaches, you have to take a boat.

Natural Wonders

Children usually respond readily to the natural beauty of the landscapes around Naples. Visiting Vesuvius (Monte Vesuvio, ➤ 14), even trekking the last stretch to the crater, is quite an adventure. Older children might enjoy walks through the Astroni woods (➤ 54) on the way to Campi Flegrei, along the Sorrento peninsula (➤ 64), or the descent from Montepertuso to Positano (➤ 69). Best of all, the whole family can enjoy exploring the grottoes on boat cruises around Capri and along the rugged Amalfi Coast, particularly the Grotta Azzurra (➤ 13) and Grotta di Smeralda (➤ 67).

Pastries and Ice-cream

Amalfi

Andrea Pansa

A difficult place to resist, Andrea Pansa has been providing amazing lemon or hazelnut pastries and totally delicious white chocolate profiteroles for years.

✉ Piazza Duomo 40 ☎ 089 871 065

Capri

Alberto

Perfect for the island's best loved ice-cream, especially chocolate, and particularly famous for its birthday cakes.

✉ Via Roma 9/II ☎ 081 837 0622

Positano

La Zagara

Superb ice-cream and pastries in a charming lemon grove; the main attraction is *granita* (iced drinks) of strawberry, lemon, almond and even fig.

✉ Via dei Mulini 6/8 ☎ 089 875 964

Sorrento

Davide

Unashamedly calls itself *Il Gelato* (*The* Ice-cream). An astonishing 60 flavours – try the excellent green apple (*mela verde*).

✉ Via Padre Reginaldo Giuiani 39 ☎ 081 807 2092

Sights

Try not to overdo it when taking children to the region's best archaeological sites: Pompei (➤ 60–1) is fine for a couple of hours, but take a good break for lunch. Concentrate on the houses and shops rather than the monuments, though it's fun to test the amphi-theatre for its acoustics. Herculaneum (➤ 58) and Paestum (➤ 68) are for real antiquity buffs and probably won't appeal to many children. Capri's Villa Jovis (➤ 57) is appreciated more for the great view than for its ruins. In Amalfi (➤ 67), try exploring the medieval arcaded passages rather than visiting the cathedral.

Price Reductions

Most national museums and other sights in and around Naples offer considerable price reductions for children – even free for under-18s at Capodimonte Museum and Museo Archeologico. Children under 12 travel at reduced fare, often half price, on most trains and ferries, free under 4. For longer trips along the Amalfi Coast, beyond Salerno, to Paestum and back, consider the *Carta Famiglia* family group-ticket, available from main stations. This gives a 30 per cent discount for a family of four travelling together. Restaurants rarely propose menus with reduced prices for children's portions, but usually accommodate specific requests, like splitting one portion between two.

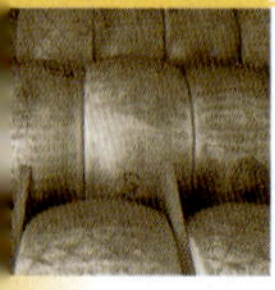

Naples

Getting Tickets
It is tough competing with Neapolitans for tickets to the opera and classical music concerts at the Teatro San Carlo and other venues. Usually your only hope at the theatre box office itself is for returns. Otherwise, your best bet is through a major hotel, with an extra commission charge, or through the town's commercial ticket agencies:

Teatro San Carlo Box Office
✉ Galleria Umberto I 15–16
☎ 081 551 9188

Concerteria
✉ Via Schipa 23
☎ 081 761 1221

Il Botteghino
✉ Via Pitloo 3
☎ 081 556 4684

MC Teatroemusica
✉ Giulio Palermo 124
☎ 081 546 2264

Classical Music

The city's classical music and opera season runs from October to June, but increasingly summer music festivals are staged in municipal parks like the Villa Comunale. Spring and autumn recitals and concerts are held in *palazzo* courtyards in the *centro storico* and the Galleria Umberto I (► 33).

Auditorium RAI-TV

The national TV network's concert hall stages both classical music and jazz.
✉ Via Guglielmo Marconi (Fuorigrotta) ☎ 081 725 1111

Bellini

Only recently resumed, dividing its repertoire between drama and opera.
✉ Via Conte di Ruvo 14 ☎ 081 549 9688 🚌 R1

Conservatorio San Pietro a Maiella

Housed since 1826 in a handsome 14th-century convent, the Music Conservatory has two concert halls, the Alessandro Scarlatti for orchestral concerts and the smaller Giuseppe Martucci for chamber music recitals.
✉ Via San Pietro a Maiella ☎ 081 459 255 🚌 R1

Teatro delle Palme

Chamber music recitals are staged here by the Associazione Scarlatti.
✉ Via Vetriera 12 ☎ 081 418 134 🚌 R3

Teatro San Carlo

One of the world's most beautiful opera houses (► 46), the theatre stages opera, ballet, and symphonic concerts played by its resident Orchestra Sinfonica and guest orchestras. The season runs from November to June.
✉ Via San Carlo 93 ☎ 081 797 2111 🚌 R2, R3

Clubs and Discos

The city's club scene changes fast. Chiaia's Piazza dei Martiri is a mob scene, Piazza Bellini lively but more sedate. *Qui Napoli* publishes up-to-date listings, but here are a few 'institutions'.

Madison Street

Naples' biggest disco caters to a trendy crowd attracted by the different theme nights – gay on Saturday.
✉ Via Sgambati 47 ☎ 081 546 6566

La Mela

More elegant than most in the fashionable Chiaia district.
✉ Via dei Mille 40 ☎ 081 413 881

My Way

An all-night establishment for non-stop dancing.
✉ Via Cappella Vecchia 30 ☎ 081 764 4735

Football

As far as religion goes, football comes just after, and for many just before, the Catholic church. In his heyday, taxis carried effigies of (now-disgraced) Argentine star Maradona next to the Madonna. You can see the Naples team, Napoli, now in Italy's Premier League, Serie A, play the best club teams in Europe in the two-tiered San Paolo stadium.
Stadio San Paolo, Piazzale Vincenzo Tecchio ✉ 081 239 5623

The Amalfi Coast

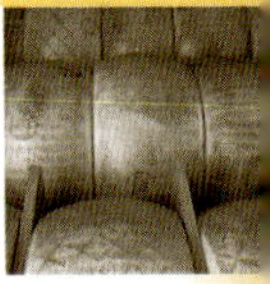

Classical Music

At Christmas and in summer the resorts outside Naples stage classical concerts and recitals in the romantic setting of their medieval churches and historic villas.

Amalfi

Cappella del Crocifisso

Recitals of sacred choral music are held in this oldest part of the Duomo, surrounded by beautifully restored 15th-century frescoes. Open-air concerts are staged on the Piazza del Duomo.

Piazza del Duomo 089 872 293

Conca dei Marini

Convento di Santa Rosa

Just west of Amalfi, this 14th-century convent perched on a ridge above the Grotta di Smeralda (► 67) hosts summer concerts of chamber music.

Via Roma 089 831 516

Positano

Santa Maria Assunta

Christmas concerts are held in the peaceful atmosphere of the old parish church.

Via Marina 089 875 480

Ravello

Villa Rufolo

The Amalfi Coast's most celebrated concerts are held in the gardens of Wagner's splendid 13th-century villa, where the German composer found the inspiration to write his opera *Parsifal* in 1877. The music, performed by major orchestras and conductors, is relayed through the streets of Ravello to create a magic atmosphere in keeping with his opera.

Piazza del Vescovado
089 857 657; (festival)
089 231 432

Clubs and Discos

Clubbing in the coastal resorts seems surprisingly more restrained than in Naples. Some of the big hotels do a bit of desultory disco, often outside on the terrace. However, only a handful of places to dance at least some of the night away can be recomended. All open around 10PM and go on much later than the hotels.

Positano

Music on the Rocks

Established favourite with the resort's habitués, this disco is down by the beach.

Via Marina 089 875 874

Praiano

L'Africana

Set in a real grotto, this disco prides itself on a hotter, more exotic atmosphere than its pirate neighbour, Il Pirata (► below).

Via Torre a Mare 089 874 042

Il Pirata

This seafood restaurant has decorated its disco as a pirate's cave.

Via Torre a Mare 874 377 377

Sailing

The Bay of Naples' major sporting event is Capri's international regatta held in May (► 86). Regional regattas may be held in summer at the major Amalfi Coast resorts – and Naples, too. For details, check with the tourist information offices at Positano, Amalfi and Naples.

Information

The tourist office provides listings of current and upcoming events, and publishes a monthly magazine for tourists, *Qui Napoli*, in English and Italian. The most up-to-date information for Naples and its surrounding region is in the daily newspaper: either Naples' own *Il Mattino*, or the national *La Repubblica*, which includes a good section for the region's cultural events.

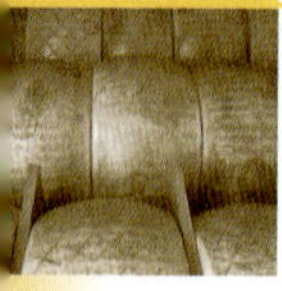

What's On When

Religious Fervour
The Neapolitans' enduring attachment to their religion shows in their enthusiastic participation in Catholic festivities throughout the year, particularly in the popular quarters around Spaccanapoli. The innocent joy of children participating in or observing the nativity ceremonies for Epiphany contrasts with the almost pagan ardour with which everybody joins in the burning of the Christmas trees 11 days later. And so it goes throughout the year, lusty merriment for the Carnival in March and then solemn observance for the Easter Passion. Only outsiders may feel like joking about the liquefaction of San Gennaro's blood in May and September (➤ 32), though in between, the July fireworks for the Madonna del Carmine are not exactly pious. As everything else in Naples, it is all gloriously ambiguous.

January
Costume Parade (New Year's Day) in the Piazza Umberto I, Capri.
Procession for Children (Epiphany, 6 Jan). Piazza del Plebiscito, Naples.
Costumed nativity play at Stazione Marittima, Naples.
Burning of Christmas Trees (17 Jan), Naples.

February
Carnival – five days of parades and parties in Capua.
Carnival – masked parades through *centro storico*, Naples.

April
Easter – renactments of the Stations of the Cross; hooded processions of lay fraternities on Sorrento peninsula.
Pasquetta (Easter Monday) – many Neapolitans take picnicking excursions out to the country.
Pizza baking contest on Naples' Piazza Mercato.
Liberation Day (25 April) – celebration of World War II invasion by the Allies.

May
Labour Day (1 May).
Maggio Sacro (first Sun) – procession from the Duomo to Santa Chiara, Naples. The first of two annual commemorations of the liquefaction of San Gennaro's blood.
International Regatta, Capri (➤ 85).

June
Open-air concerts – start of the summer season of classical music in the courtyards of Castel Nuovo, Castel Sant'Elmo and Castel dell'Ovo, Naples.
Jazz concerts in Ravello.

July
The Wagner Festival commemorates the composers residence at the Villa Rufolo, Ravello (➤ 85).
Madonna del Carmine is celebrated by fireworks at Piazza Mercato, Naples, simulating the burning of the campanile.
Midnight concerts – start of the summer arts season featuring music, films and cabaret in the public parks.
Sant'Anna (25 Jul) – procession of illuminated boats for the patron saint of Ischia.

August
Ferragosto (15 Aug) – Assumption Day festivities include music and games throughout Naples.

September
Theatre, music and dance season at the Palazzo Reale in Caserta.
Pizza festival in Naples.
San Gennaro's Feast Day (19 Sep) – the second commemoration of the liquefaction of the saint's blood in the Duomo, Naples.

October
Start of the autumn classical music season at the Conservatory and *palazzo* courtyards, Naples.

November
Opera – opening of Teatro San Carlo's opera season, Naples.

December
There is a Christmas market on Via San Gregorio Armeno, Naples.
There are general seasonal festivities throughout the *centro storico* in Naples.

Practical Matters

Police control the sometimes chaotic Naples traffic

TIME DIFFERENCES

GMT	Italy	Germany	USA (NY)	Netherlands	Spain
12 noon	→ 1PM	→ 1PM	← 7AM	→ 1PM	→ 1PM

BEFORE YOU GO

WHAT YOU NEED

● Required
○ Suggested
▲ Not required

Some countries require a passport to remain valid for a minimum period (usually at least six months) beyond the date of entry – contact their consulate or embassy or your travel agent for details.

	UK	Germany	USA	Netherlands	Spain
Passport	●	●	●	●	●
Visa (Regulations can change – check before your journey)	▲	▲	▲	▲	▲
Onward or Return Ticket	▲	▲	▲	▲	▲
Health Inoculations	▲	▲	▲	▲	▲
Health Documentation (➤ 91, Health)	●	●	▲	●	●
Travel Insurance	○	○	○	○	○
Driving Licence (national)	●	●	●	●	●
Car Insurance Certificate (if own car)	○	○	○	○	○
Car Registration Document (if own car)	●	●	●	●	●

WHEN TO GO

Naples

High season / Low season

	JAN	FEB	MAR	APR	MAY	JUN	JUL	AUG	SEP	OCT	NOV	DEC
Season	Low	Low	Low	Low	High	High	High	High	High	Low	Low	Low
Temperature	6°C	6°C	10°C	13°C	17°C	22°C	25°C	25°C	21°C	16°C	11°C	6°C
Weather	Cloud	Cloud	Cloud	Wet	Sun	Sun	Sun	Sun	Sun	Cloud	Very wet	Wet

Very wet · Wet · Cloud · Sun

TOURIST OFFICES

In the UK
Italian State Tourist Board
1 Princes Street
London W1R 8AY
☎ 020 7408 1254
Fax: 020 7493 6695

In the USA
Italian Government Travel
Office (ENIT)
630 Fifth Avenue
Suite 1565
New York NY 10111
☎ 212/245 4822
Fax: 212/586 9249

Italian Government Travel
Office (ENIT)
12400 Wilshire Boulevard
Suite 550
Los Angeles, CA 90025
☎ 310/820 1898
Fax: 310/820 6357

CONSULATES

UK	Germany	Netherlands	Spain	USA
081 663 511	081 761 3393	081 551 3003	081 761 4013	081 583 8111

WHEN YOU ARE THERE

ARRIVING

The main entry point for Naples and the Amalfi Coast is Naples' Capodichino Airport ☎ 081 709 111. There are bus services every 50 minutes to Naples city centre 6AM to midnight (CLP ☎ 081 531 1646), and two buses, morning and afternoon, to Sorrento (Curreri ☎ 081 801 5420).

MONEY

The Euro is the legal currency of Italy. Euro notes come in denominations of 5, 10, 20, 50, 100, 200 and 500. Coins are 1, 2, 5 bronze-coloured Euro cents and 10, 20 and 50 gold-coloured Euro cents. In addition there is a 1 Euro coin with a silver centre and gold surround and 2 Euro coin with a gold centre and silver surround. 1,000 lira = 0.52 Euros.

CUSTOMS

From within EU for personal use (guidelines)

800 cigarettes, 200 cigars
1 kilogram of tobacco
10 litres of spirits (over 22%)
20 litres of aperitifs
90 litres of wine, of which 60 litres can be sparkling wine
110 litres of beer

From a non-EU country for your personal use:

200 cigarettes OR
50 cigars OR 250g of tobacco
1 litre of spirits (over 22%)
2 litres of intermediary products (eg sherry) and sparking wine
2 litres of still wine
50g of perfume
0.25 litres of eau de toilette
The value limit for goods is 175 Euros.

Under 17s are not entitled to the tobacco and alcohol allowances.

Drugs, firearms, ammunition, offensive weapons, obscene material, unlicensed animals.

OPENING HOURS

○ Shops
● Offices
● Banks
● Attractions/museums
● Post offices
● Pharmacies

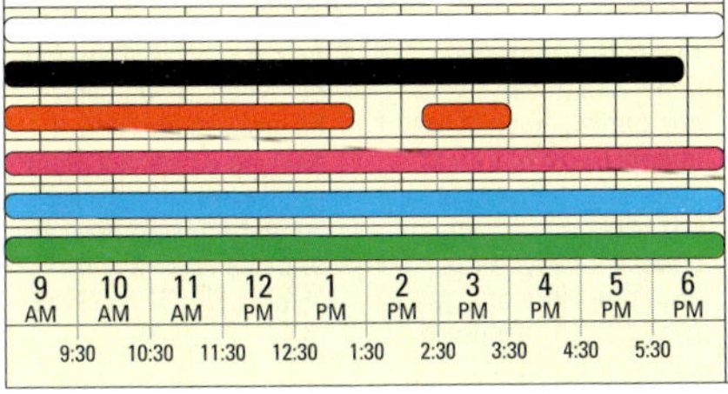

Shops in winter open 3:30 to 7:30PM. Department stores and shops in tourist areas may stay open all day and sometimes later in the evening. Some shops are closed Monday morning, others on Saturday afternoon or all day. Most close on Sunday. Banks are closed during lunch (usually 1:20–2:20). They are closed weeekends. Museum times are erratic and should always be checked for changes.

POLICE 112

FIRE 115

AMBULANCE 113

DRIVE ON THE **RIGHT**

TOILETS **CHARGE**

DRIVING

Speed limit on motorways (autostrade), for which there are tolls: **130kph**

Speed limit on main roads: **110kph**; on secondary roads: **90kph**

Speed limits on urban roads: **50kph**

Must be worn in front seats at all times and in rear seats where fitted.

Random breath-testing is frequent. Limit: 80mg per 100ml of blood.

Petrol is cheaper in Italy than in Britain and many other European countries, and diesel (*gasolio*) tends to be cheaper than unleaded (*senza piombo*). Outside urban areas petrol stations open 7AM to 12:30PM and 3 to 7:30PM. Credit cards are rarely accepted.

In the event of a breakdown, ☎ 116, giving your registration number and type of car and the nearest ACI (Automobile Club d'Italia) office will assist you. You will be towed to the nearest ACI garage. This service is free to foreign-registered vehicles or cars rented from Rome or Milan airport.

PUBLIC TRANSPORT

Internal Flights Services throughout the country are provided by the national airline Alitalia's associated company Minerva (reservations ☎ 147 865 641; Capodichino ☎ 081 709 333). The flight time to Naples from Rome is 60 minutes and from Milan 75–85 minutes.

Trains Italian State Railways (Ferrovia dello Stato, or FS) have improved enormously in recent years. The Intercity train reaches Rome from Naples in 2 hours and the Treno Eurostar 15 minutes faster. Trains provide good service around the Bay of Naples, the Circumvesuviana to Pompei and Sorrento, and the Cumana to Pozzuoli and Baia.

Regional Buses There is no national bus company, but SITA (☎ 081 552 2176) provides a good regular service between Naples (Via Pisanelli, near Piazza Municipio) and the Amalfi Coast resorts all the way to Salerno. In the other direction, SEPSA buses (☎ 081 542 911) leave Piazza Garibaldi for Pozzuoli and Baia.

Boat Trips Ferries and the much faster hydrofoils leave from two main piers in Naples' harbours. From Molo Beverello, Caremar (☎ 081 551 3882) serves Capri, Ischia and Sorrento. Alilauro (☎ 081 761 1004) serves Ischia from Mergellina. Capri is also linked directly to both Positano and Sorrento.

Urban Transport City buses are cheap, charging a flat fare. Invariably you need a ticket before getting on. Buy them in a *tabacchi* or from kiosks at bus terminals and stops. In Naples, most routes pass by the Stazione Centrale.

CAR RENTAL

Car hire is available in most cities and resorts from international and Italian companies, but it is not cheap. Generally local firms offer better rates but cars can only be booked locally. Air or train travellers can get special inclusive deals.

TAXIS

Taxis are available in all towns and tourist resorts. They can be hailed, though you'll be lucky to find one passing when you want it. Otherwise find a rank (at stations and *piazze*), or call a radio taxi (in Naples ☎ 081 552 5252 or 081 556 4444).